DEATH, THE FINAL FRONTIER

PREQUEL to *The Merciful Law of Divine Synchronicity*

OREST STOCCO

DEATH, THE FINAL FRONTIER

copyright © 2016 by OREST STOCCO

All rights reserved. No part of this book may be reproduced or transmitted in any form or by any means without written permission of the author.

ISBN 978-1-926442-14-3

Edited by Penny Lynn Cates
Cover Design by Penny Lynn Cates

"Fate is the death we owe to Nature.
Destiny is the life we owe to soul."

*BONE: A Journal of Wisdom,
Strength, and Healing*

Jungian Analyst
Marion Woodman

"I have failed in my foremost task: to open people's eyes to the fact that man has a soul and there is a buried treasure in the field and that our religion and philosophy are in a lamentable state."

Letter to Eugene Rolfe,
Nov. 13, 1960

C. G. Jung

Note to the Reader

Nobody wants to die. No, that's not true. There are people in this world who want to die for one reason or another, but generally speaking, we don't want to die. Why?

If asked, what would you answer? "I'm not ready to die yet." That's what most people would say. And many would say, "That's a stupid question!" Each answer would reflect a person's feelings; but there's a depth to this question that no one can explore, because it goes to the very purpose of our existence, and who knows what this purpose is?

Death is all around us today. So much so that it seems we have become inured to it; but not quite so. We still fear death, despite seeing it practically every day on TV with another shooting or terrorist attack on innocent people. We cannot get away from it no matter how hard we try, or wherever we go. Death is here to stay.

Until science can figure out how to extend our life indefinitely, we're all sure to die; and not unless we have come to terms with our life and are ready to meet our maker (if we believe in the concept of a personal creator) will we die with peace of mind. This, then, was my inspiration for writing this book—to ameliorate the fear of death and dying.

A tall order. But that's what writers do. We explore the mysteries of life and hope to come to some resolution. As with all of my books, I was called to write this book to share my thoughts on death, the final frontier of life; but in all honesty, I did not expect it to take me where it did—to the very precipice and purpose of our existence.

"What do I do now?" one asks, as they stare into the abyss. It's terrifying to stare into the face of death, and no one wants to; but death cannot be avoided, so I took the challenge and wrote my thoughts on the final frontier of life just to see where my creative unconscious would take me, and I invite you to join me on this incredible journey, which will continue with my twin soul sequel *The Merciful Law of Divine Synchronicity,* the story of my relationship with my guiding principle.

Orest Stocco
Georgian Bay, Ontario
Sunday, July 31, 2016

CONTENTS

1. SERENDIPITY CAME CALLING 1
2. MY CRISIS OF FAITH 4
3. MY EDICT OF SELF-DENIAL 8
<u>INSERTED CHAPTER:</u> THE SYMBOL OF MY LIFE TO BE 12
4. MY LIFE OF EXILE 19
5. MY SISYPHEAN ROCK 22
6. THE PURPOSE OF LIFE 26
7. THERE IS NO ONE WAY 30
8. MY FIRST NOVEL 34
9. MY PERSONAL SHADOW 38
10. MY ORACLE 41
11. THE STORY OF OUR BECOMING 45
12. THE MYSTERY 50
13. MY REGRESSION TO THE BODY OF GOD 54
14. THE IVAN ILYCH PROBLEM 61
15. SOLVING THE IVAN ILYCH PROBLEM 65
16. THE GUIDING PRINCIPLE OF LITERATURE 72
17. THE SILENT MESSAGE OF LITERATURE 78
18. THE FEAR OF DEATH 87
19. THE GREAT RECONCILIATION 92
20. LET`S TALK TURKEY 97
21. THE FIG TREE THAT JESUS CURSED 103
22. THE DIVINE MADNESS OF EROS 112
23. MEMORIES AND THE SELF 117
24. HOW MUCH PROOF DO WE NEED? 125
25. THE IRONY OF OUR BECOMING 129
26. THE WINNING RUN 136

1. SERENDIPITY CAME CALLING

"Synchronicity can point us to new challenges or teach us what we need to know..."

I didn't expect to write about my thoughts on death, but serendipity came calling *Saturday, April 9, 2016* when I was nudged to go to Chapters in Barrie for Psychologist Teresa DeCicco's signing of her new book *Living Beyond the Five Senses*: *The Emergence of a Spiritual Being,* and by happenstance I met Jeanne Van Bronkhorst at the same table as Teresa signing her own new book *Dreams at the Threshold* which offered guidance, comfort, and healing for those about to cross over to the other side and those that are left behind.

It happened innocently enough, as it always does when *the omniscient guiding principle of life* whispers into our ear to do something we are called to do to fulfil our destined purpose, and being familiar with these little whispers when they come to me I had to pay close attention; but the more the coincidences piled up—reviews of Sandra Martin's new book *A Good Death*: *Making the Most of Our Final Choices,* new legislation permitting doctor-assisted suicide, an alarming number of suicides in the community of Attawapiskat in Northern Ontario, and other telling signs on death and dying—the more the idea for a personal account on death gestated until it sprouted with the title, *Death, the Final Frontier.*

But I had trepidations. Not that I didn't want to accept my new creative challenge, but because my views on death would be so radically different from society that I wondered if it was worth my bother; and so, as I often do, I consulted my personal Oracle for advice—

"Tell me Padre," I said to St. Padre Pio in my mind (this is a dialectical exercise in what C. G. Jung called "active imagination" which I've been practicing ever since I wrote my novel *Healing with Padre Pio* four years ago. It's a creative technique that engages the unconscious with the conscious mind; but whether it's the spirit of St. Padre Pio, an archetypal figure, or my "superior insight" I do not know), "is this idea worth investing my time and energy into? I'd have to interrupt writing my new book *The Merciful Law of Divine Synchronicity*, which I don't want to do because it's taken this long to catch the rhythm of my story; but I'm very intrigued about exploring death from my personal point of view. Any thoughts, Padre?"

"*Thank you for asking. Yes, I do have a few thoughts on the subject. As you know, you wouldn't be called were it not necessary for you to expand upon the subject of death from your unique perspective; but given your appetite for writing books, a short interruption won't interfere with your new book on synchronicity.*"

St. Padre Pio was a humble Capuchin Monk born in the village of Pietrelcina in southern Italy, north of where I was born in the village of Panettieri in Calabria, and I got to know St. Padre Pio intimately when he was channeled for my novel *Healing with Padre Pio* by a very gifted psychic medium (I also read a dozen biographies on Padre Pio's remarkable life during my ten sessions with the psychic); but that's precisely what I mean when I say that my views on death would be too radical for public consumption, which is why I wanted to consult my Oracle before continuing—

"You can see where this is going already. Won't a book on death from my personal perspective scare the bejesus out of people?"

"*On the contrary. The world is crying for a new perspective on death. How long can the world go on pretending that that is all there is to life? People are tired of the guessing game when the anecdotal evidence for life after death is so vast and comprehensive that it would be foolish for one to believe that death is the end of life. Don't be intimidated by your project. You've been down this road before. Trust your creative instincts and let the chips fall where they may. They always do anyway, don't they?*"

"True enough. But we do have choices, and it's my choice to continue with this new project or to complete my book on synchronicity first. This is why I'm consulting you."

"*I can speak for one who has crossed over, and my input would be invaluable to your new project on death; so if you would like to make our relationship a part of your creative inquiry into the final frontier of life, I'd be happy to oblige.*"

"Won't our relationship tax the reader's credulity?"

"*Readers are much more sophisticated than you give them credit for. The world isn't what it used to be. It's no longer black and* white. It's fifty shades of grey, if I may be allowed to borrow the phrase from one of your contemporary best-selling authors."

"In a different context, of course?"

"Not necessarily. Life is life, regardless the context. That's the problem with human nature, always categorizing behavior and labelling it. Man has many dimensions, and not until he realizes the fullness of his being will he stop fearing to cross the final frontier."

"Death, you mean?"

"Yes. How can man embrace death when he has labelled it the end of life? Life does not end with death. Life continues after death, as the stories in Jeanne Van Bronkhorst's book Dreams at the Threshold show. Only by expanding one's paradigm on death and dying can the fear of death be removed; that's why you were called to write this book."

"Thank you, Padre. I'll get back to you as I need you…"

2. MY CRISIS OF FAITH

"Dreams pave the way for life..."

I was born into a Roman Catholic family in southern Calabria, Italy; and my Roman Catholic faith was vital to my understanding of life and death.

According to my faith, I was born with the stain of original sin upon my soul, and Jesus died on the cross to wash away the stain of original sin and save me from damnation; but somewhere in my teens I began to feel uneasy with my faith, and inspired by Maugham's novel *The Razor's Edge* in high school I became a seeker like Maugham's hero Larry Darrell, and I began to explore what the philosopher Socrates called the "secret doctrine."

"There is a doctrine uttered in secret that man is a prisoner who has no right to open the door of his prison and run away," said Socrates in Plato's *Phaedo*; and by "secret doctrine" the gadfly of Athens meant reincarnation, the belief that when we die we come back to live life over again; and this, of course, went against my Roman Catholic faith.

My faith taught me that we only live one lifetime, that my immortal soul was created at the moment of my human conception, and when I died I would go to heaven or hell, or maybe purgatory—a concept I never could understand. Jesus was my savior, and to avoid going to hell forever I had to die in a state of grace, which meant that I had to die without the stain of mortal sin upon my soul. And to remove the stain of sin upon my soul, both mortal and venial, I went to confession every Saturday or Sunday morning before Mass, and sometimes in the middle of the week as well; such was my fear of going to hell.

I did everything I could to be true to my faith, and even thought of becoming a priest to help safeguard my salvation; but something happened when I discovered reincarnation, something that took me years to understand but which had immediate consequences. I began to feel suffocated by my faith, and I panicked. And that's when I began to have past-life recollection dreams that eased the anguish of my constricting faith.

A past-life recollection dream is not like any other dream. It is an actual memory of a past lifetime, but this recollection happens while one is sleeping; hence the name, "past-life recollection dream," and while in high school I had four of these special dreams.

In one dream I was in England. I don't know which century, but I was a fish monger peddling fish with my wooden cart shouting *"Kippers! Fillets!"* I don't remember much else of this past lifetime, but I cannot dismiss the feeling that it was me in another body in another country in another century, and I can still smell the stink of fish as if it were yesterday.

In another dream I was a North American Indian. My recollection of this past lifetime is so vivid that I can still feel the pain I had to endure during my rite of passage into manhood, a ritual that I refused to go through when I was first summoned by our chief because I did not have the courage and was cast out of the village to live on my own until I had enough courage to go through my rite of passage, and I grew in my manhood and became chief of my village. My name was "Bear Claw," which I had earned by killing a bear with my knife. The bear mauled my face, and I had a scar for life. But I was a good and fair chief for my tribe, and I remember being counseled by our tribal shaman. This dream left such an impression upon me that I can still smell the lingering odor that hung over our wigwam village.

But the dream that most affected me was my dream of being a black slave in southern Georgia. I was known as Solomon, the Good Slave; and I tried to escape from the plantation not once, not twice, but three times. The third time I was taught a lesson that changed my life forever. During one of my Sunday morning whippings I awakened to my immortal soul and realized that my master could own my body but not my soul, and this newfound freedom gave me the courage to endure all of the pain and suffering inflicted upon me. This lifetime changed my karmic destiny, because I *knew* that I had an immortal soul and would never die.

In my fourth past-life recollection dream I was in ancient Greece. I was an aristocrat and statesman whose counsel was sought out and highly respected, and I remember that we were preparing to defend our noble city from an imminent invasion, and although I don't remember exactly what I said to the men that were called in from the fields to defend our city, I said something to the effect, "Remember, you are Athenians. When you kill, do not kill with the savagery of barbarians, but with the might and dignity of your noble bearing."

I was in high school when I had these dreams, and despite not knowing that these dreams were recollections of my past lives, they affected me deeply; and a few years later I read Jess Stearn's book *The Search for the Soul: Psychic Lives of Taylor Caldwell,* and I knew that one day I would write a book on my own past lives, which I did when Penny and I relocated from my hometown of Nipigon in Northwestern Ontario to Georgian Bay, Southcentral Ontario where serendipity introduced me to a past-life regressionist and I had seven regressions that inspired my novel *Cathedral of My Past Lives*. This is why my perspective on death is so radically different from most people. But before I continue with my personal history, I'd like to consult with my Oracle...

"Tell me Padre, if you would please—I'm consulting you because I need to know something about these dreams I had in high school. I hope you don't mind. Were these past-life recollection dreams prompted by *the omniscient guiding principle of life*? I ask because I've come to believe that our life is divinely choreographed despite our free will (it took me years to resolve this paradox), and I've come to see that when one is ready to break the karmic cycle of life and death they will be called to the sacred knowledge of the secret way of life; or am I getting ahead of myself here?"

"No, you are not getting ahead of yourself. What is the final frontier of life after all if not the rebirth of soul into another body? And what is the purpose of reincarnation if not to realize your destined purpose? But as you came to realize in your own journey to wholeness and completeness, man must complete what nature cannot finish. And when life has made one ready to take evolution into their own hands, the way opens up to them. That's why you had your past-life recollection dreams. You were ready for the final frontier—"

"Yes, I know that; but where did my dreams come from?"

DEATH, THE FINAL FRONTIER

"From your inner self. But at this point in our dialectic on death you would be wise to get an objective confirmation for a comprehensive definition of dreams. By this I mean from a source outside the creative parameters of this book. I would suggest your mentor."

"Who? Certainly not my literary mentor?"

"No, not Hemingway. Doctor Jung."

"Of course. Give me a moment, please; I know which book to consult…Okay, I found it. It's from Jung's book on dreams. From the Bolligen Series, with a forward by Jungian scholar Sonu Shamdasani. "My dreams," said Jung, "are the speech of my soul." And he goes on: "Dreams are the guiding words of the soul." I've come to believe this too, Padre; but Jung answers my question very nicely when he says, **"Dreams pave the way for life, and they determine you without understanding their language."** And he goes on to say something which is worth noting: "One would like to learn this language, but who can teach and learn it?" These quotes are from Jung's *Red Book*. Shamdasani quoted Jung for his forward to Jung's book on dreams, and I could not have asked for a more satisfying definition. Dreams are the language of the soul, and they guide us whether we're aware of it or not; and soul is our inner self as you implied. That's what you were getting at, wasn't it? And that's why I relied upon my dreams for my book *The Summoning of Noman*. I let my dreams guide me to unravel the symbolic message of my *daemonic* poem 'Noman' that I wrote in high school and which shocked my English teacher. But that's getting off topic. I just wanted to know what you had to say about my past-life recollection dreams."

"I think we said what needed to be said for your reader to catch a glimpse of the big picture. This is the challenge of this book. You have to part the veil of life and give your reader a glimpse of soul's purpose in the world. Death is not the end of life; and if I can be of any assistance in your endeavor to prove this, please call upon me anytime."

"I will. Thank you, Padre."

3. MY EDICT OF SELF-DENIAL

"I take the clue divine..."

I don't remember ever doubting the existence of God, and I even remember one experience I had in my early teens when I was kneeling in my darkened bedroom holding my right hand in the air and saying, "God, I can't see you like I can't see my own hand, but I know that you are there like I know my hand is there and one day I will see you."

I had a sense of inner knowing of God's existence, which I could never prove; but this kind of knowing does not need to be proven because it just *is*. This is the kind of gnostic knowing that C. G. Jung demonstrated when he was asked by John Freeman in the famous BBC *Face to Face* interview if he believed in God and Jung replied, with a sweet smile and twinkle in his octogenarian eyes: *"I know. I don't need to believe, I know."*

But where does this kind of knowing come from if not from one's inner self, one's immortal soul which is a spark of divine consciousness? And if we are all sparks of divine consciousness, why do only some of us have this sense of inner knowing of God's existence and not others? What is this difference between the knower and the doubter?

When I studied philosophy at university when I came back from Annecy, France where I had gone to begin my quest for my true self, I was taken by the intellectual integrity of some of the world's great thinkers, but I could not fathom how they could be so adamant in their belief that God did not exist, like two of my favorite philosophers, Jean Paul Sartre and Albert Camus, whose understanding of the human condition had a great influence upon my thinking because what they had to say about life resonated with my own experience.

But how could this be? How could their unbelief in God resonate with my belief in God? That was incomprehensible. And yet, that's how I felt about their philosophical positions on the meaninglessness and absurdity of life, and it took many years before I resolved the inherent contradiction of my paradoxical nature.

I *knew* that Sartre was right when he said, "I am what I am not, and I am not what I am," but I also knew that man was not a "useless passion" as Sartre proclaimed; there had to be purpose to our life that neither Sartre nor Camus could fathom, and that's when serendipity came to my aid by inspiring a fellow student to give me P. D. Ouspensky's book *In Search of the Miraculous* that introduced me to Gurdjieff's teaching, and I dropped out of university in my third year to forge my own path in life.

Like Francis Thompson's poem "The Hound of Heaven," when I caught the scent I had to follow it. *"Rise, clasp My hand, and come!"* God shouted, and I had no choice but to drop out of university when Gurdjieff's teaching caught hold of me, and I got a job in the bush camps where I had worked in my youth, and then I started my own house painting business that I expanded to include drywall taping which I did for more than thirty years.

But what was it about Gurdjieff's teaching that compelled me to drop out of university to forge my own path in life if not my sense of inner knowing that his teaching was right for me despite my reservations about his premise that man is not born with an immortal soul? As hard as I tried, I could not explain why Gurdjieff's teaching attracted me, and it wasn't until I went for a walk one day in my second year at university when I created my *Royal Dictum* that Gurdjieff's teaching finally opened up to me.

I was standing on the breakwater that divided the Nipigon River from the marina that fateful day when I looked up into the heavens and said, *"God, I know that we get nothing for nothing in this world, or any world for that matter; so please tell me, what price truth?"*

I was desperate. Philosophy had failed to answer my questions, and I could not make any headway with Gurdjieff's teaching despite my inexplicable attraction for it; and as I waited for God to reply I stared at the fast-flowing waters of the Nipigon River, which for some strange reason brought to mind the Preacher's words in *Ecclesiastes*: "All the rivers run into the sea; yet the sea is not full; unto the place from whence the rivers come, thither they return again." I stared transfixed in thought as the river flowed past me.

And then, again for whatever divine reason, Sophocles' play *Oedipus Rex* came to mind and the price that King Oedipus paid to save his kingdom: true to his edict to banish whoever was responsible for the blight upon his kingdom, which his blind soothsayer Tiresias revealed to be Oedipus himself, he gouged out his eyes and exiled himself from his kingdom to atone for killing his father and defiling his mother's bed, and I took out my pocket notebook and wrote my own edict of self-denial, which I called my *Royal Dictum*: ***"I am like Oedipus Rex. I am going to exile myself out of my own kingdom. I embrace my becoming blindly, and I leave all of my sins behind me. I am going to go against the natural course of evolution, and each obstacle that I encounter, I will consume."***

By whatever divine logic, the Preacher's words in *Ecclesiastes* and the play *Oedipus Rex* symbolically meted out the price that I had to pay for the truth I sought from God, because I felt that I could get to the source of my true self by exiling myself out of the kingdom of my own senses (the pleasures of life); that's what inspired my edict of self-denial that I called my *Royal Dictum*, and I stepped off the breakwater onto the mainland and threw away my package of cigarettes and began my exile from myself...

"Do you mind, Padre? I have a strong urge to engage you, given the emotional gravity of my *Royal Dictum*. Philosophy wasn't satisfying the desperate longing in my soul, and I couldn't make headway with Gurdjieff's teaching. I was desperate, and I had nowhere to turn. Is that why I was 'inspired' to create my *Royal Dictum*?"

"This was the turning point of your life. Once again, your inner self came to your rescue, as it always does when one comes to an impasse on their journey to wholeness. Philosophy opened up the way for Gurdjieff's teaching to come into your life by way of Ouspensky's book, but you did not have enough momentum to break into Gurdjieff's teaching; that's why your inner self inspired your Royal Dictum. You needed this edict of self-denial to create a powerful head of steam to break through into Gurdjieff's teaching, which is not an easy teaching to break into. Many seekers have taken up the Gurdjieff Work, but few have reaped the benefits of this

teaching. You did, thanks to your Royal Dictum. If I may draw a comparison with my own life—"

"Please don't! I know what you're going to say, and it would be a presumption to compare the sacrifices that I made living my *Royal Dictum* with what you had to suffer living the Holy Wounds of Jesus. No, please don't Padre."

"That was my cross, which I chose to bear as you chose to bear the cross of your Royal Dictum. But every person's cross is always relative to one's need, and to compare one person's sacrifices with another would not be fair to the individual. All I wanted to say was that you reaped the reward of your Royal Dictum as I reaped the reward of my stigmata. It's not a question of who suffered more; it's always a question of the individual soul's need. I needed to suffer as I did to satisfy the longing in my soul—"

"Again, pardon my interruption. Shouldn't we be clear on what this reward was? Or should I wait and let the dialectic of this story reveal this in its own time?"

"There's no harm in telling your reader that the reward we are referring to is what I called 'my glory' and you called 'virtue.' This is the special energy that soul needs to satisfy its longing for wholeness, which your Royal Dictum granted you in abundance."

"As did your stigmata, only a million times more!"

"Yes, but as I said; that's what I needed."

"Okay, I get it. But I get the feeling that we're forcing the dialectic, and I don't want to overwhelm the reader. Why don't we just let the story unfold on its own?"

"As you wish...."

INSERTED CHAPTER

THE SYMBOL OF MY LIFE TO BE

"The mandala signifies the wholeness of the self..."

I really don't know if I should even mention this, but it is so central to the story of my becoming that it gives symbolic context to my whole journey of self-discovery, and I feel I have no choice but to reveal my incredible experience. All the same, I'm going to consult my Oracle because I know St. Padre Pio will appreciate my literary predicament...

"I have to smile at my quandary, Padre. It is so rich in irony that I don't know what to say; but I have to reveal my experience of the symbolic squaring of the circle of my life in my second year of philosophy studies at university a few days before I went for my walk on the breakwater where I was inspired to create my *Royal Dictum* that changed my life forever, because my experience that night in my bedroom symbolically manifested *my life to be*. Would you believe that I completely forgot to mention this experience and brought our dialectic on the final frontier of life to resolution with my closing chapter "The Winning Run" when it occurred to me yesterday while sitting in the shade of the maple tree in our front yard reading *Jung and the Lost Gospels* by Stephan A. Hoeller that I had completely forgotten to mention the experience I had of the symbolic squaring of the circle of my life in my bedroom that night at university after I threw Ouspensky's book *In Search of the Miraculous* down on my desk out of sheer frustration because I couldn't make heads or tails out of Gurdjieff's teaching of 'work on oneself.' So here I am now, inserting this chapter in between chapters 3 and 4 to tell the story of the experience that foretold *my life to be*. Can you believe it, Padre? It's like I have come back from my future to correct my past. Isn't that ironic, given what Jesus said to Glenda Green about our life not being stuck in a linear structure? I've come back to my own story to give my story more meaning with the experience I had of the

DEATH, THE FINAL FRONTIER

symbolic manifestation of squaring the circle of my life; meaning, doing the impossible and transcending myself to realize my immortal nature. Who would believe that my unconscious manifested a mandala symbol of a blue circle squared by a yellow light to reveal to me the profound depths of my unconscious need to find my true self and prove to me that I would do the impossible which in Gurdjieff's words would be "creating" my own soul—if I can express it this way. Can I, Padre? Do you understand what I'm trying to say?"

"You've taken a long time to get to the point, but yes; I understand perfectly, and it is fitting that it happened this way. It was meant for you to bring this book to closure before you revealed your experience of the symbolic squaring of the circle, because this will prove in a literary sense that life is not stuck in a linear structure; that we can return to our life story from any point in time to better align our story with its divine purpose. So, please share the experience. It will be a welcome addition to your already-completed story, and it will give your reader something to ponder as he proceeds to read your story knowing that it has already been written. By all means, share your experience my friend."

"This is really bizarre, Padre! I don't think I've ever read a book where the author inserts a chapter after he has completed his book and tells the reader that he has done so, but won't this throw the reader into confusion?"

"Some may be confused, but on the whole your readers will find your story more compelling and by revealing your experience of the symbolic squaring of the circle it will make it more intriguing. After all, you did forget to include this experience; and if you stop to think about it, how could you possible forget this momentous experience? It was the symbolic manifestation of your life to be in your journey of self-discovery, and by all accounts it was meant to be included in your story. Why do you think you forgot?"

"I can only guess."

"Please do."

"As you know only too well, I abandon to my creative unconscious when I write; and in my abandon, I rely entirely upon my creative instinct to find my story's direction. I'm not entirely without input, but as to the flow of the story I give that entirely to my creative instinct, and I guess I got so caught up in the flow that it never occurred to me that I had left out the most vital experience of my becoming—the symbolic squaring of the circle of my life. But for what reason did I forget?"

"*To give your story more depth, more meaning, more intrigue. Readers love intrigue. Did you know that mystery novels are the biggest selling genre in the world?*"

"I didn't know. But I can see it. We all love a good mystery."

"*And what greater mystery can there be in life than the mystery of the self? Every person has asked or will ask the question 'WHO AM I?' This is the intriguing element of your story, and you were meant to forget this most vital piece of information until you brought your story to resolution. This information inserted now between chapters 3 and 4 will only add suspense to your story, and readers love suspense.*"

"Having said that, it's only fair to reveal what I experienced that night in my bedroom of the house I shared with three other men; a married ex-police officer who had come to university to get a law degree; a bookkeeper who had come to university to get a teaching certificate; and a supply school teacher who needed a place to stay for the school term, and whose mother also happened to be one of my English teachers in high school. So here it is, Padre; the incredible experience of the symbolic manifestation of my life to be—"

"*Pardon my interruption, but before you relate your experience please explain what you mean by your life to be.*"

"Certainly. Well, I had no idea that I would be dropping out of university in the second semester of my third year because philosophy would have brought me as far as it could take me in my journey of self-discovery and I had to go out into the world to forge a new path with Gurdjieff's teaching, so the symbol of the blue circle squared by the yellow light that appeared to me out of thin air that night in my bedroom was confirmation from my unconscious that I would do the impossible and transcend myself by 'working' on myself with Gurdjieff's teaching which I had not yet penetrated. That's why I threw Ouspensky's book down onto my desk in frustration. I just didn't 'get it,' and I shut the lights out and lay on my bed in abject dejection. Here's what I think happened, Padre; and please tell me if I got it right. Will you?"

"*Certainly.*"

"Okay. I was in my second year of philosophy studies and I had already begun to sense that the path of philosophy was not going to take me where I had to go to find my true self, and this put a lot of pressure upon my psyche; that's why I think my unconscious responded with the symbol of the circle of blue light squared by a yellow light, just to let my conscious mind know that I would resolve my predicament—"

"What predicament? Please explain."

"My predicament was that when I came back from France where I had gone to begin my quest for my true self I went to Lakehead University in Thunder Bay, just an hour's drive from my hometown of Nipigon, to study philosophy to find an answer to the two most haunting questions of my life—*who am I?* and *why am I?* Now, I should explain that the second question did not occur to me until my unconscious revealed my need to know *why I am* with a dream I had one night in Annecy, France where I had gone to begin my quest for an answer to the question *who am I?* In my dream one night I left my body and entered into the mind of every person in the world, and I took every question that every person in the world had ever asked and reduced them all to one question, *why am I?* And it took me years to find out why I had this dream and what this question meant. My unconscious manifested this dream to let me know that this question *why am I?* is the central mystery of our lower self, or ego personality; and the question *who am I?* is the central mystery of our essential self. So I went to France to look for an answer to *who am I?* and while in France I had this dream that awakened me to the central mystery of my ego personality, *why am I?* That's why when I came back from France I went to university to study philosophy, because I believed that philosophy was the mother of all disciplines and would give me an answer to the two most haunting questions of my life; but as I said, I began to sense in my second year that philosophy wasn't going to answer these questions, which is why I believe my unconscious manifested that mystic mandala to let me know that I would resolve my dilemma in *my life to be*, which I did when I dropped out of university the following year to forge a new path with Gurdjieff's teaching of 'work' on myself—and, of course, with my *Royal Dictum* that I did not even know I would be living by because I would not be inspired to create my edict of self-denial until a few days after this miraculous experience in my bedroom that night. Does that explain why I think I had that experience that night?"

"As convoluted as it sounds, it's perfectly clear when looked at closely; which I know your readers will do because you've caught their attention now. Please relate your experience and let your reader be the judge of whether this actually happened to you or whether you made it up for reasons which not even I could possibly fathom—"

"You do make me laugh, Padre! But that's precisely why I hesitated to relate this experience, because it's so unbelievable. But then, I've read enough biographies on your life (as well as on Carl Jung who also had experiences that defy credulity. Not as miraculous as yours, but experiences that cautioned him to keep them to himself until the end of his life, which is why he never published *The Red Book* in his lifetime); so my experience of the mandala that symbolically manifested *my life to be* won't sound so incredible in light of yours and Carl Jung's. But I'll just have to see, won't I?"

"Trust your readers, my friend."

"There I was then, in my darkened bedroom; alone again (*God, there can be no loneliness like the loneliness of a seeker who hits a brick wall!*), full of anger at myself for not being able to break into Gurdjieff's teaching—there was a secret to his teaching which pulled me in like a giant magnet, but it wouldn't reveal itself to me; and I lay on my bed with my hands behind my head stewing in my own juices, and that's when the miracle happened, if I can call it a miracle—which I did for many years until I discovered C. G. Jung who offered me a much more plausible explanation with his insight into the mandala symbols that the unconscious manifests to give expression to one's psychic state, and my psychic state needed resolution so badly that my unconscious manifested before my eyes in my pitch black bedroom a tiny dot of blue light that stayed suspended in mid-air for a moment or two and then expanded to create a circle of blue light about three feet in diameter, looking like a donut with a hole in it; and a moment or so later, a dot of yellow light appeared at the top of the circle of blue light, within the circumference, and then it formed a straight line of yellow light within the blue circumference, stopped, made a right-angled turn, and made another straight line, stopped, made another right-angled turn, and continued with another straight line, and finally one more straight line to form a perfect square of yellow light within the circumference of the blue circle; and the 'squared circle' stood suspended in mid-air long enough for me to let me know that I wasn't dreaming or hallucinating, and then it disappeared before my eyes. There you have it, Padre; that's the mandala symbol that my unconscious manifested for me to see the tension that I was experiencing in my soul and the resolution that I would realize in *my life to be* after I created my *Royal Dictum* that would open me up to Gurdjieff's teaching of 'work on oneself' which would become the path I needed to find my true self."

"You are correct to believe that this symbolic manifestation of the 'squared circle' was a psychic confirmation of finding your true self, and if you choose to call it a miracle no one would object—"

"I object! For many years I attributed the manifestation of my 'squared circle' symbol to the 'Blue Light' of the Spiritual Leader of that New Age Religion of the Light and Sound of God that I took up after Gurdjieff's teaching had done all it could for me, because the leader of this New Age Religion had led us all to believe that he was also our Inner Master, which was a concept I never could buy into because I believed that our Higher Self was our Inner Master (and still do), and it wasn't until I began to study C. G. Jung that I saw my mandala experience as a manifestation of my own psyche and not an intercession from some divine agency; but I have to share something else with you now before I forget, something that may just help to add to the credibility to the incredible story of *my life to be*."

"You have already given your readers much too ponder, given that your story has already been brought to closure, and this new information will only add another layer of intrigue. But I agree, you have to share the experience you had with Gurdjieff, because this speaks to another aspect of the dreaming process that your readers should be aware of."

"I think so too. Okay, I dropped out of university in the second semester of my third year and got a job in the bush camps where I had worked in my youth, and I brought my *Royal Dictum* and Gurdjieff's teaching of 'work on oneself' with me; and in a dream one night I met Gurdjieff and asked him if he would accept me into his inner circle of students. He replied to me, 'You not ready yet.' But after two years of 'working' on myself with my *Royal Dictum* and Gurdjieff's teaching, I met Gurdjieff in a dream again and asked him if I was ready to be admitted into his inner circle, and I saw myself in the center of a circle of his inner students with me kneeling and Gurdjieff standing over me, and he placed his hands upon my shoulders and said, 'You ready now,' and I became a member of his inner circle. And when three years later I gave birth to my immortal self in my mother's kitchen, I knew that Gurdjieff's teaching had done all it could for me; that's when serendipity introduced me to that New Age Religion that I lived for over thirty years before I learned what I had to learn from this teaching and then dropped it to live my own path, which I do with joyful abandon in my writing. Enough said, Padre."

"Now we can resume with the story."

"Yes, my life of exile…"

4. MY LIFE OF EXILE

"Suffering is the essential nature of all paths to God..."

    No one would believe me if I told them, but on the breakwater that day I vowed to live my *Royal Dictum* for the rest of my life; but in three and a half years my commitment to deny myself the pleasures of life had resolved the paradoxical consciousness of my *being* and *non-being* enough for me to transcend myself, and I no longer had to live my edict of self-denial because my *Royal Dictum* had served its purpose of bringing me to my true self just as Jesus promised: "For when the master himself was asked by someone when his kingdom would come, he said, **"When the two will be one, the outer like the inner, and the male like the female neither male nor female."**

    Or, if I may express my self-transcendence in the language of philosophy, I completed Sartre's incomplete dialectic of becoming and wrote in my one of my notebooks: **"I am what I am not, and I am not what I am: I am both, but neither: I am Soul."**

    But I need respite here, because memories of my life of exile have overwhelmed me yet again, and to ease my anxiety I'm going to consult my Oracle because no one suffered more for their cause in this life than the humble Capuchin Monk Padre Pio—

    "Permit me, Padre; you suffered the stigmata for fifty years, so you know more about the virtue of suffering than anyone. Could you please say a few words about what Gurdjieff called *intentional suffering*, because I fear I may not do this concept justice?"

    "Suffering was my glory, and as you already know from reading all those biographies on my life, I could not get enough of suffering—"

    "Didn't you say somewhere that you wanted to intoxicate yourself with pain?"

    "Your memory serves you well. Yes, I did say that; and I meant it. Why don't you look up the passages on my suffering and quote my exact words?"

"I will…"

For the next few hours I went through my biographies and found what Padre Pio had to say about the eternal agony of his suffering in Renzo Allegri's book *Padre Pio, Man of Hope*: "On *August 5, 1918*, while he was hearing the confessions of his seminary students, Padre Pio had a mystical experience that he described in the following terms to his spiritual director: 'I was filled with extreme terror at the sight of a heavenly Being who presented himself to the eye of my intellect. In his hand he held some kind of weapon, like a long, sharp-pointed steel blade, which seemed to spew out fire. This Being hurled this weapon into my soul with all his might. It was only with difficulty that I did not cry out. I thought I was dying…Since that day I have been mortally wounded. I always feel in the depths of my soul a wound that is always open and that causes me continual agony…The wound is so painful that it is enough to cause one thousand and one deaths'" (*Padre Pio, Man of Hope*, by Renzo Allegri, pp. 72-3). And I also found the passage in *Secrets of a Soul, Padre Pio's Letters to his Spiritual Directors* where he said in one of his letters upon receiving the holy wounds of Jesus, "I want to intoxicate myself with pain." But I have to inquire further—

"Okay, I found the passage when the heavenly Being pierced your soul with his steel blade of fire, and I'd like to ask you a question which may seem rather odd, but I'm strongly nudged to ask it: as real as your experience was, given your eternal agony, can this piercing of the heart also be symbolic? And by this I mean that whenever a soul steps onto the path of God it is pierced in the heart by the Holy Blade of Fire and begins the transformation of the self through suffering. I may not have articulated my thought well, but I want to know if your life is the extreme example of one's life on the path to God, or am I being too vain in my presumption?"

"No, it is not vanity that inspires your question; it is a genuine desire to understand the divine nature of suffering, which you understand much better than most souls on the path to God. Yes, you are correct to say that my life was an extreme example of la via de sofferenza, which in English simply means the way of suffering, which is the essential nature of all paths to God; but we must put this

DEATH, THE FINAL FRONTIER

suffering into its proper perspective, otherwise your readers will flee from the path to God like bats out of hell—"

I broke into laughter. Padre Pio has an incredible sense of humor, which I experienced many times writing my novel *Healing with Padre Pio,* and which I love because it resonates with my own sense of humor (this is why he said in one of my spiritual healing sessions with the psychic medium that we were very much alike); and when I stopped laughing, I said: "I asked, because my *Royal Dictum* was my path of suffering; and not to compare it with your path—*God forbid the presumption!* —I suffered enough to initiate myself into the secret way of life; and that's what impelled me on the path to God."

"Well said. Yes, you initiated yourself into the secret way of life with your Royal Dictum and Gurdjieff's teaching of conscious effort and intentional suffering, and especially with his technique of non-identifying with the objects of your desire—the very essence of the path of pure intentions; but let's explain what we mean by divine suffering before we get sidetracked, as we have a tendency to do in our discourses. Give me your definition of divine suffering and I will add my two cents worth—"

Again, I laughed. "You sell yourself short, Padre! Alright, let me give you what I learned about divine suffering. All suffering, and specifically *intentional suffering,* is divine by virtue of the transformative power of what Jesus called 'making the two into one.' Jesus is speaking esoterically. By two he meant our inner and outer self. Suffering transforms our *being* and *non-being* into what St. Paul called a "new creature." This "new creature" is the spiritual self born of the mystical marriage of our *being* and *non-being*; and suffering is divine because it is God's way of giving us the grace to transcend ourselves through the natural process of life experience. Life entails suffering, because this is the way of life; but suffering is divinely purposive, which is why Jesus said to Carl Jung's spiritual guide Philemon in Jung's *Red Book,* "I bring you the beauty of suffering." In a word, Padre; Jesus knew that suffering rejoins soul with God. That's why Jesus died on the cross. His crucifixion was symbolic of man's reunion with God."

"Well said, my friend. Let's leave it there for now, shall we?"

"Fair enough..."

5. MY SISYPHEAN ROCK

"One must die before dying..."

There may be some people in this world who are not afraid of dying, though I doubt very many, and there are definitely people who welcome death for one reason or another which, no doubt, inspired Camus to write, *"There is only one really serious philosophical question, and that is suicide,"* but I happen to believe that life is not meaningless and absurd as the Algerian philosopher concluded, and it didn't matter to me how many times Sisyphus had to roll his rock up that hill, I could never imagine him happy.

Albert Camus' analogy of the myth of Sisyphus with man's futile and hopeless labor can be summed up in the street-rich saying, "You work hard and then you die." But that's an old and tired cliché, which the Preacher in *Ecclesiastes* expressed much more eloquently when he said: *"Vanity of vanities; all is vanity. What profit hath a man of all his labor which he taketh under the sun?"* That's what I sought to answer...

I didn't go into a monastery to live my life of self-denial; I took my *Royal Dictum* out with me every morning when I went into the marketplace to work my trade in the house painting business that I had started shortly after I dropped out of university, and I told no one about my edict of self-denial because that would have been foolish.

But strangely enough, this worked for me instead of against me, because the more I denied myself the pleasures of life (this took enormous effort that I could not show, which I did by virtue of Gurdjieff's techniques of *self-remembering* and *non-identifying* with the objects of my desire), the more I created a mystique about myself (to the point where a rumor began to circulate in my hometown that I was gay because I didn't date women); and this, I began to see, pulled more energy into my field that I needed to grow into my true self.

The truth is, I had no idea what I was doing; but I knew that what I was doing was right for me, because this was the price I had to

DEATH, THE FINAL FRONTIER

pay for the truth I sought from God; and the truth I sought was my true self, which I felt I would find at the headwaters of my life.

By exiling myself out of the kingdom of my own senses, I felt I would get closer to my true self; and the more I denied myself the pleasures of life, the more I began to "see" the sacred meaning of Christ's cryptic teaching, until one day I saw the truth behind his most paradoxical saying, *"He that loveth his life shall lose it; and he that hateth his life in this world shall keep it unto life eternal"* (John, 12: 25).

"One must die before dying," say the Sufis, which sums up Christ's whole teaching of salvation; but salvation from what, if not from the consciousness of our false self? That's what Gurdjieff's teaching did for me, and why I was attracted to it without understanding its essential purpose of "creating" my own immortal soul.

Gurdjieff believed that man is not born with an immortal soul, but with his teaching one could "create" his own soul; and despite my reservations about the basic premise of his teaching (I had an inner *knowing* that I had an immortal soul from my past lifetime as Solomon, the Good Slave), Gurdjieff's teaching attracted me because I *knew* that it was what I needed to find my true self, which I had promised to find from the day I had a traumatic sexual experience that shocked my conscience awake because I knew that the person who did what he did that night was not me. It was me, but not me; and I vowed to find out who this other "me" was that did what he did that night or I would die trying.

This other "me" was my false self, the unresolved karmic matrix of all my past-life personalities; but I've told this story already in *The Summoning of Noman,* and again in *Gurdjieff Was Wrong but His Teaching Works,* so I need not expound upon it here; suffice to say that my quest for my true self began with my *Royal Dictum,* which initiated me into the secret way of life that opened me up to Gurdjieff's teaching and Christ's sayings and parables. That's why my perspective on death is so radically different, because I "died" to myself to "find" myself, and I no longer fear crossing the final frontier…

"Again, Padre; I have to engage you in a discourse, because I fear I have stepped into the deep end of the pool much too quickly for my reader's comfort. As you know, when I sit down to write I abandon to my creative unconscious—well, that's not entirely true. I do, and I don't. It's paradoxical. Zen-like. Doing without doing. But to engage what C. G. Jung called the "transcendent function," one has to engage his imagination without losing control to his imagination, something like this discourse with you: I engage you, but at the same time I cannot lose my autonomy to you; fair enough?"

"Well said, my friend. Yes, I know how difficult and exciting the creative process can be when one engages their transcendent function. But as you came to see, one has to trust one's Muse to find its own aesthetic purpose. Your story has already been ensouled with its divine directive, and you do your creative spirit justice."

"Then you don't think I've taken the readers beyond their depth?"

"As you have learned to trust your Muse, you must learn to trust your readers. The quickest way to win their confidence is to treat them as equals. A reader would rather be puzzled by a writer's work than to be talked down to."

"I'm not so sure about that. I've tested my readers with my spiritual musings, and I'm not so sure they can be trusted. I learned this from Gurdjieff. He said that every person has what he called a 'chief feature,' which is the defining characteristic of one's false personality; and if one pushes this button, which I had a tendency to do with my spiritual musings, one upsets the reader because they don't want to be revealed. That's why writers write fiction. It's much safer. So, Padre; did I go too far? Is this where my story wants to go?"

"No journey is without risk. This is as true for writing as it is for life. Every book has its own risks, and the risk you take writing this book is revealing something that the reader may not be ready to hear. But you don't know who is ready and who is not. Didn't you write a spiritual musing called 'The Eleventh Person'? This was your way of saying that your books are not for everybody. But how do you know who the eleventh person is?"

"I don't. No one knows but God. And when one is ready, they are called."

"As you were called to Gurdjieff's teaching. Ouspensky's book was marked by God to find you, but you had to go to university to be in the right place to receive it. And so will it be with this book. It is already marked for those who need to read it."

"I can confirm this with how I got to work with you for my book *Healing with Padre Pio*. I would never have met the gifted psychic whom you had chosen to guide in her work as a spiritual healer had I not moved to Georgian Bay, but I was ready for the next stage of my journey through life; that's why I was called to have a spiritual reading by her, which only confirmed what I had long begun to suspect that our life is divinely choreographed. Just as I was called to write *Healing with Padre Pio,* so are people called to read the books they need to read for their own journey through life; but we can talk about this another time, if the dialectic of our story deems it. For now, I just want to be clear on where this book is going. I don't want to go half way and find out it's not meant to be."

"It's meant to be. I assure you."

"That's all I needed to hear..."

6. THE PURPOSE OF LIFE

*"The sole purpose of human existence
is to kindle a light in the darkness of mere being..."*

Albert Camus ends his essay *The Myth of Sisyphus* in the vain hope that "the struggle itself towards the heights is enough to fill a man's heart." "One must imagine Sisyphus happy," he said; but how can Sisyphus be happy condemned to such drudgery for eternity?

How can one be happy stuck in a dead-end job, if one has a job at all that is given how precarious the marketplace can be, or stuck in a soul-crushing relationship? This is why Camus saw life as meaningless and absurd, because he could not see the purpose of all this Sisyphean drudgery; but just because he couldn't see it doesn't mean it wasn't there.

I could not rebel against life as Albert Camus, which he did with such literary eloquence that he won the Nobel Prize for Literature in 1957 *"for his important literary production, which with clear-sighted earnestness illuminates the problems of the human conscience in our times,"* because I *knew* deep within that life had purpose; but I had no idea what this purpose was, and my quest for my true self became a quest for life's inherent purpose.

Gurdjieff opened the door to the inherent purpose of life with his teaching of "work on oneself," because with his teaching I could "create" my own soul, and that was purpose enough for me despite my reservations about the basic premise of his teaching; because the more I "worked" on myself, the more life's purpose revealed itself to me. But this is such a difficult concept to convey that I have to consult my Oracle to give it clarity—

"Padre, I just finished rereading *Padre Pio, The Stigmatist*, by Rev. Charles Mortimer Carty, and I'm half way through *Padre Pio, Man of Hope* by Renzo Allegri, which I read one or two times already, and once again I'm moved to tears by what you had to go through to be true to your spiritual calling, all of that pain and suffering because of the Holy Wounds of Jesus that you invited upon yourself, not to mention your bad health and all those years of persecution that your detractors inflicted upon you because of their envy of your saintliness; but I have to ask you something about human nature, because I really am puzzled by man's behavior. Why, I keep asking myself, are people so blind in their own vanity? Albert Camus, and Jean Paul Sartre for that matter, two philosophers I deeply respected, could not see the logic of life, so they had to create a philosophy to give life meaning; but all they did was justify their own enormous vanity. It seems to me that they wanted to pour the whole ocean into their tiny tea cup, and that to me is the true absurdity of the human condition."

"You do make me laugh, my friend. Yes, there is a great irony here. But you make a good point about human nature. My only response for now, because later we may get into this more deeply, is that these men chose the mind over faith; but the mind cannot fathom the mysterious depths of God's creation—"

"Pardon my interruption, Padre; but if I'm not mistaken I highlighted something you said about faith in one of the books I just read. Let me look it up, if I may."

"By all means..."

Okay, I have it. It's in *Padre Pio, The Stigmatist,* page 104. You said—or, I assume it was you, and you will have to verify this because in this case it was an "inward voice" that whispered to Professor G. Felice Checcacci of Genoa— "Faith is not to be argued over, either you accept it with your eyes closed, admitting the inadequacy of the human mind to understand its mysteries, or you reject it. There is no middle way. The choice is up to you." First of all, was that you that said this? And second, can you expand upon that?"

"I see you haven't changed much since we talked through the medium who spoke for me for your novel Healing with Padre Pio; *you continue to ask the hard questions. Let me answer this with a question of my own, if you will permit me?"*

"Certainly."

"When Doctor Jung found his spiritual guide in Philemon when he explored the depths of his own unconscious with what he later came to call an exercise in 'active imagination,' as we are doing now, what did he end up calling Philemon?"

"I see where you're going with this. Jung was both troubled and fascinated by the figure of Philemon in his unconscious, and it took him a long time to come to terms with his inner guiding principle; but in the end he referred to Philemon as 'superior insight,' and by this he meant his Higher Self. So what you're trying to tell me in your own modest way, is that Professor Checcacci's 'inward voice' was his own spiritual guide, or Higher Self?"

"Before I answer that, please provide the context of what the Professor's inner voice said to him. Without context, what the voice said won't mean half as much."

"Okay...Professor Checcacci was an unbeliever. He lived in the Orient for some forty years and he studied many religions. When he returned to Italy, he read about Padre Pio and was impelled to go and see you. This is what he wrote in a letter: "Tormented and obsessed by my studies in comparative Oriental religions, I finally fell into the heresy of considering Christianity to be a derivation of Brahmanism and Buddhism..." And then the Professor read a booklet by Del Fante called "From Doubt to Faith," and he was so moved that he had a dream of you. And you said to him, "Come and see me." He did not go to see you, but three months later you showed up in his dreams again and said, "I waited for you, but you did not come." One would think this would've been enough for him to go and see you, but he didn't; so you appeared to him one sleepless night and said to him, "If you cannot come, write." He was so shaken by the vision of your presence that he jumped out of his bed, but by then you had disappeared. The next morning, he wrote and asked you for peace of soul; and two days later he felt a sudden start and a voice said to him, "Go to church and pray." It had been thirty years since he had been in a church, but he went; and as he was praying, the 'inward voice' whispered to him what I quoted about faith. So, I ask you again Padre; was the 'inward voice' that spoke to him your voice?"

"Now that we have the context for the Professor's experience, what I said to him about faith makes much more sense. Yes, it was my voice. But as you correctly deduced with your own journey to your true self, one's inner voice and the omniscient guiding principle of life are one and the same thing. But I choose to call it Divine Spirit."

"Yes, I know; but it takes a long time to see that this spark of divine consciousness that we are all born with and Divine Spirit are one and the same thing. One has to grow and evolve in the consciousness of one's divine nature to realize this. And that, if I may be allowed to say so, is what the purpose of life is all about—***the individuation of Divine Spirit!***

"Enough said. We'll talk again when necessary."

"When I have need of superior insight, you mean?"

"You do make me laugh, my friend..."

7. THERE IS NO ONE WAY

"All paths lead to the self..."

"This life is the way, the long sought-after way to the unfathomable, which we call divine. There is no other way, all other ways are false paths," wrote C. G. Jung in *The Red Book*, the chronicle of his "confrontation with the unconscious."

When I read these words in *The Red Book* my heart leapt with joy, because Jung had just confirmed my own experience with the secret way of life that is the impulse of our *becoming*; but I would never have discerned this had I not "worked" on myself with my *Royal Dictum*, Gurdjieff's teaching, Christ's sayings, and every life-wisdom saying that I grafted into my personal ethic that would help me find my true self.

That's the gift that Gurdjieff's teaching gave me, the realization that to find my true self I had to *become* my true self, which I did by "creating" my own immortal soul with *conscious effort* and *intentional suffering*.

Gurdjieff called his teaching "work on oneself," but it took years of reading and writing to work out the logic of self-transformation through this special kind of "work," and I would never have resolved Gurdjieff's misperception had I not experienced what I did when I had seven past-life regressions when Penny and I moved to Georgian Bay, because in one of my regressions I experienced myself as an embryonic un-self-realized soul in the Body of God before I was sent into the world to grow and evolve in my divine nature, and I experienced the actual dawning of my reflective self-consciousness in my first primordial human lifetime as the alpha male of a small group of higher primates, and from lifetime to lifetime I continued to grow in my own individuality until I *became* my true self, which put the lie to Gurdjieff's premise that we are not born with an immortal soul.

Gurdjieff was wrong in his premise but correct in the execution of his teaching, because as one "works" on oneself one *becomes* one's true self, and it is this *becoming process* that Gurdjieff misperceived to be the "creation" of one's own immortal soul which his teaching precipitated, because *becoming* one's true self awakens one to their divine nature. So, what exactly does it mean to *become* one's true self? Let's see what my Oracle has to say...

"The irony of your life Padre, was that in your lifetime as the Holy Stigmatic whose obedience to the Pope and the Holy Mother Church was absolute, you deemed teachings like reincarnation heretical, and you weren't especially fond of the Jehovah's Witnesses and communist teachings either, nor did you approve of Masons and women wearing short dresses, often scolding penitents during confession; but when we talked through the psychic medium for my novel, you answered all of my hard questions but one. I won't mention what question that was, but you did acknowledge that sin in itself does not exist and certainly does not condemn one to hell, because all of life is an experience in the individuation of Divine Spirit from one lifetime to the next until we realize our divine nature, and you did tell me that there is no one way because all ways are expressions of the one Way; but I'm calling upon your superior insight to help me clarify this concept of *becoming*. Can you spare a couple of cents worth of divine wisdom for me, please?"

"You do have a way of pushing the envelope. But you wouldn't be you if you didn't. And that, ironically, is the essential wisdom of man's becoming. It's all about pushing the envelope and expanding one's boundaries, because one cannot grow in a closed system. Yes, I was closed-minded about some teachings in my cloistered lifetime. But that's what I needed to grow in my own individuality. As I said in one of our sessions with the medium who spoke for me, life is a journey of self-discovery; and we all grow according to our own needs. If soul needs a certain teaching, then that's the teaching that it will be attracted to, and no one teaching is better than another because all teachings lead soul back home to God."

"It's a good thing that this is only an exercise in active imagination, because if people were to believe that you actually said this—"

"What does it matter which container pours out wisdom—archetypal Padre Pio. Divine Spirit, or me? Superior insight is superior insight, is it not?"

"True. Why am I being so cheeky this morning?"

"Because you're tired of skinning the same cat. Don't worry about the outcome, just go where your creative spirit takes you and let God take care of the rest."

"Fair enough. Alright, let's talk turkey then. This whole concept of *becoming* our true self through the natural process of life experience, would you like me to offer an explanation before you offer your two cents worth?"

"Please do."

"Simply put, life creates the consciousness of man's *being* and *non-being*, or inner and outer self if you will; but not only does life create the self of our *being* and *non-being* through personal experience, it also resolves the self-consciousness of our *being* and *non-being* into a self-consciousness that is both *being* and *non-being* but neither; it is the transcendent consciousness of our divine nature, which is our soul self, and this transformative process defines our *becoming*. But this is the natural process of our *becoming*, which can only take us so far to our true self. This is why Gurdjieff said that nature can only evolve us so far and no further. To complete what nature cannot finish and *become* our true self, we have to take evolution into our own hands; which is what "work on oneself" is all about and what Jesus meant my making the two into one. Have I got the gist of it?"

"You have described the archetypal pattern of soul's growth through life, and I don't have much to add to that. But I will say one thing for now, and that is this: man grows in his spiritual nature according to his desires—"

"Whoa! Let's not go there just yet. I know that all roads lead to Rome, but some roads are much safer than others. Let's concentrate on these first, shall we?"

"Didn't you write somewhere that the shortest way to God is through hell?"

"Yes, I did; but I meant the hell of one's own shadow."

"I agree. But one grows in one's identity according to one's desires, and in the growth of one's desires one creates one's own

shadow. I make no judgment on one's desires. All I am saying is that one must learn to be discerning in one's desires."

"I guess I jumped the gun. Sorry, Padre. You're right, we live and die by our desires; and it makes no difference what they are, because they are all fodder for our *becoming*. But who would understand this? It's much too esoteric for most people."

"Didn't I say that your readers are more sophisticated than you give them credit for?"

"You did. Okay, can we leave it here for now?"

"Just one more thing. I owe everything to my cloistered lifetime as a Capuchin friar, and I wouldn't trade that lifetime for anything in God's universe. It made me what I am, and if I were asked to live that life over again I would happily do so."

"Not me! I came back to live my life over again, which I didn't know I did until you told me; but living my same life twice is enough for me, thank you!"

"You do make me smile. But let's leave this concept of parallel lives for another time, shall we? I think your reader has enough for now."

"Agreed. Until we talk again, then…"

8. MY FIRST NOVEL

"Memoir is the facts of life.
Fiction is the truth of life..."

I wrote something in my first novel *What Would I Say Today If I Were to Die Tomorrow?* that offended my reader's sensibilities (actually, my novel upset my hometown of Nipigon, Ontario much more than Thomas Wolf's novel *Look Homeward Angel* offended his hometown of Asheville, North Carolina, and Penny and I relocated to Georgian Bay for peace of mind): "The first thing I would say if I were to die tomorrow would be this: **We live more than one life, and it is foolish to deny this simple truth**; and the second thing that I would say is that **self-deception is our greatest threat to personal growth, happiness, and wholeness.**" I wrote this fifteen years ago; and if anything, I am more convinced of this today than I was when I wrote it.

I wrote this novel because I was suffering from *life fatigue*, a phrase that I coined at the time to describe how much it had cost me to find my true self; and although the idea for my first novel was set free by Ruth Picardie's memoir *Before I Say Goodbye*, I was so tired of life that I had to tell my unbelievable story before I died.

Ruth Picardie was diagnosed with cancer and was given one year to live, that's why she wrote her memoir *Before I Say Goodbye*; so I put myself under the fabled Sword of Damocles and wrote *What Would I Say Today If I Were to Die Tomorrow?* Like Ruth Picardie, I too wanted to say what I had to say before I died; but why was it so upsetting?

It took me a few years to work it out, but when all is said and done I had to accept the simple fact that people don't want to hear the truth about their life, and my first novel, modeled upon my own life, shone the light upon my community shadow and revealed the false side of human nature which, to my horror, offended everyone.

That's how naïve I was, though; because like our eminent Canadian writer Alice Munro said to Shelagh Rogers in a CBC radio interview before receiving the Nobel Prize for Literature, "Memoir is the facts of life. Fiction is the truth of life," and I chose to write fiction to get to the truth of life because I knew enough to realize that fiction gave the writer much more latitude than memoir, which Munro confirmed by a comment she made about her own fiction when she was asked by Shelagh what her hometown thought of her writing, "I don't know," replied Munro; "they don't speak to me."

But this only confirms that **self-deception is our greatest threat to personal growth, happiness, and wholeness** because until one owns up to their own shadow they will always be conflicted and never become the person that they are meant to be...

It's a long, long journey to one's true self as the Sufi Poet Attar's allegory *Conference of the Birds* illustrates with the wisdom of soul's journey back home to God (out of thousands of birds that began their quest for God, only thirty completed the quest and got to look into the Face of God), a book that I loaned to one of my customers, along with *Spiritual Literacy, Reading the Sacred in Everyday Life* by Frederic and Mary Ann Brussat, because my healthy but strong-willed septuagenarian customer wanted to read something that would help guide her on her own spiritual journey because she was in crisis with her Christian faith, and had been for many years and only went to church for the sake of propriety; but try as I may, not once in all the talks that we had over tea in her cozy kitchen whenever I painted her house or dropped by for a visit could I get her to see the undeniable reality of causative behavior.

"I don't believe in karma," she would insist, and then puff on her cigarette in her tar and nicotine filter holder; and I would make the same argument—

"But hasn't science proven that nicotine causes cancer?"

"Yes," she would reply, grudgingly.

"Well, smoking causes cancer; that's karma. There's nothing mysterious about karma, May; it's all about cause and effect. You have a problem with reincarnation, that's all."

"Oh, you and that kooky Shirley MacLaine! I don't believe in reincarnation!"

And so it went, year after year. That's why when I dropped out of university to forge my own path in life I promised to look wherever my path took me, because I had no desire to get stuck like May Tyler. But letting go of one's beliefs can be harder than staring into the face of one's mortality; that's why the Sufis say that one has to unlearn what one has learned to gain the sacred knowledge, which gives meaning to their saying that to gain salvation one has to die before dying, and all this has to do with the false side of our personality that I brought to light in *What Would I Say Today If I Were to Die Tomorrow?* May Tyler spotted her own shadow in my novel; and, well, compound that with all the other characters in my novel who saw bits and pieces of themselves and one can understand why my community was so upset with me. But these memories have made me anxious—

"Padre, would you mind discoursing with me a while to help relieve some of this anxiety that all of these memories have given rise to?"

"This was the most troubling time of your life, and your loved one's life as well, but which you both needed to prepare you for the next stage of your journey to wholeness. I welcome the opportunity to talk with you. What specifically would you like to talk about?"

"How in God's name did I get myself into that fix? I'm still puzzled by how devastating my book was to my community. Good God, Padre; it was like I had murdered the town's only child or something. I couldn't believe how vitriolic my community could be."

"In a very real sense, you did murder your town's only child by exposing your community's shadow personality in your novel. You shocked your community psyche by holding up a mirror to its dark side, and the town turned against you and your loved one. But you're not the first writer to experience the Archetypal Shadow's vengeance. Do you think Dante had an easy time of it when he wrote The Divine Comedy? Who do you think he modeled his characters on if not real people? No one wants to see their dark side, but that's what writers do. They seek the truth of life, and whoever gets caught in their sight is in for a real surprise. You did what you were called to do my friend, and it got you where you needed to be to continue on your journey of self-discovery. Just be thankful that you came out of this experience in one piece."

"But nobody will ever know the price that Penny and I paid to get here, unless I write a novel on this experience, which I hope to do one day. I've already got the title. *We May Be Tiny, but We're Not Small.* We live in Tiny Township, and my title is a play upon smallness of character; but I don't know if I'll ever get to write it. Will I, Padre?"

"Yes, you will write it. It will be one of your best novels. But you have other books to write first, starting with this one. Do you have any more concerns?"

"One more question, if I may?"

"Certainly."

"I don't want this to sound like more than what it is, but I would like to know if the publication of *What Would I Say Today If I Were to Die Tomorrow?* altered the course of my community's karmic destiny? By raising the consciousness of my community's dark side, did my novel shift the community's destiny?"

"The short answer is yes. Your novel broke the hold that your community shadow had upon the psyche of your community, and everything changes when the dark side is brought to light because once seen it can never be unseen. This is how the soul grows. You may have offended your community with the truth, but you did your town a great service."

"Which no one appreciates but you and me!"

"There you go again, doubting the intelligence of your readers. You really must do something about this—"

"Alright! I hear you! Let's leave it there, shall we? But I do thank you for getting me out of that foul mood my memories got me into. Until we talk again, then."

"*Ciao for now, my friend...*"

9. MY PERSONAL SHADOW

"The conflict between who we are and who we want to be is at the core of the human struggle..."

"The shadow by nature is difficult to apprehend. It is dangerous, disorderly, and forever in hiding, as if the light of consciousness would steal its very life," wrote Connie Zweig and Jeremiah Abrams in their introduction to *Meeting the Shadow, The Hidden Power of the Dark Side of Human Nature*; but I would never have become aware of my own shadow had I not experienced what I did one lonely night in my bedroom when I hit a brick wall with Gurdjieff's teaching of "work on oneself" after I dropped out of university. Before I tell the story of what alerted me to my own shadow however, let me say a few words about the shadow first to give my strange experience the context it deserves...

The shadow is the unconscious underside of our ego personality, and even though we are not conscious of our shadow it grows in tandem with our personality; and over time our shadow takes on an identity of its own just as our ego personality.

This insight into the unconscious shadow side of our personality has inspired writers like Dostoevsky to write *The Double*, Robert Louis Stevenson to write *The Strange Case of Dr. Jekyll and Mr. Hyde,* and Oscar Wilde to write *The Picture of Dorian Grey.* These novels dramatize the existence of the repressed and unpleasant side of our personality; but as clearly as we can see the shadow side of the personality in these novels, it takes great moral courage to see our own shadow, and very shocking when we do.

By the time I wrote *What Would I Say Today If I Were to Die Tomorrow?* I had developed a sixth sense for seeing the shadow; not only my own shadow, but other people's shadow as well; which was why my novel disturbed the people of my hometown. And as painful as this lesson was for me (it gave me great comfort to learn over the years how many writers were despised for basing their characters on real people, like my literary mentor Ernest Hemingway), it was worth it to learn just how painful it can be for a person to see their own shadow in a work of fiction, because no one wants to be seen for what they are not but pretend to be.

But that's what the shadow is, the false side of our ego personality. It is everything that we don't want the world to see about us. It is the unconscious side of our personality that we create out of all those little experiences that humiliate us, that part of our psychic make-up that we feed with all the lies we tell and all our little vanities and grotesqueries that we refuse to acknowledge and own up to; and our shadow grows according to the values that we live by, which I wasn't aware of until I began living Gurdjieff's teaching.

But I hit a brick wall with Gurdjieff's teaching, because as much as I had grown in what Gurdjieff called my "work self," I came to a dead stop; and I stopped growing because I came up against the impenetrable wall of my own shadow. That's when I had the strange experience of hearing a voice in my mind that was to propel me to new heights of growth and understanding, a voice that said to me: *"Why do you lie?"*

I was sitting in my bedroom, feeling dejected and miserable. I was living my *Royal Dictum* and "working" on myself with passionate commitment, but for some inexplicable reason I stopped making progress, feeling like all of my efforts had taken me as far as I could go, and I didn't know what else I could do to get to the headwaters of my life.

I felt so dejected that I put on the most inspiring piece of music that I had to lift my spirits, Beethoven's Ninth Symphony; and I can't be certain of this, but I believe I heard the voice in my mind ask me *why do you lie?* when the final movement, *Ode to Joy*, came to a bombastic, mind-exploding climax; and I was startled into awareness.

I heard the question *"Why do you lie?"* clearly and distinctly. It was a male voice, and I waited for it to say something else; but that was all it said. The music stopped, and I sat in silence totally perplexed. Finally, I said: *"Why do I lie? I don't lie; I'm a truth seeker."* And I waited. But the voice did not reply. Not then, not ever.

Not audibly, anyway. But the power of that question shattered my self-image so badly that it gave a whole new meaning to

Gurdjieff's techniques of *self-remembering* and *non-identifying;* and I paid such focused attention to my thoughts, my words, and my behavior that I caught my private devil by the tail and redeemed myself from my unconscious falseness.

That's how I came face to face with my own shadow…

10. MY ORACLE

"We all have superior insight..."

Had I not experienced what I did to reclaim myself from my shadow, Jung's comment that it takes great moral courage to see one's own shadow would not have meant much to me when I discovered Jung through his memoir *Memories, Dreams, Reflections* that opened up a whole new world of possibilities for me because Jung's psychology provided a conceptual framework for the individuation process that I was living with my *Royal Dictum*, Gurdjieff's teaching, Christ's sayings and parables, and all the wisdom sayings that I had gathered from life; and the first chance I got, I drove to Thunder Bay and purchased *The Portable Jung* (I don't remember exactly, but I think I bought it at Coles), edited by Joseph Campbell, and to this day Carl Gustave Jung continues to guide me with the gnostic wisdom of his writing...

"So, Padre; if I may consult you now, let me ask you—God, it's taken a long time for me to ask you this question; possibly because it never occurred to me before, but why now? Was I not ready yet, as you said to me when I asked the hard question? No, don't answer. That's self-explanatory. We cannot take in more than we can absorb, right?"

"If by that you mean that you would not understand because you do not have enough life experience to understand, then yes. When you asked me about whether Jesus died on the cross or not, you could not possibly understand the truth of Christ's crucifixion. It was beyond your ability. I suffered the Holy Wounds of Jesus for fifty years, and I still marvel at the mystery. But that's for another time. Now ask me your question."

"Was it your voice that spoke to me in my bedroom that night? You did say that you and I had arranged to meet in this lifetime (through my psychic medium, that is), and that you would assist me in my life's mission; was that you assisting me by asking me the question *Why do you lie?* That question was so potent it sent me into warp drive in my quest for my true self, because I suddenly realized that I had to reclaim myself from my false self to get to the headwaters of my life. That's how I became aware that one does not find his true self but *becomes* his true self by reclaiming himself from his false self, only then can one grow in the wholeness of his divine nature. Am I correct in this?"

"Essentially, yes. And to answer your question, it was me who spoke to you that night because I felt your sorrow so deeply I had to intercede. The depth of your vanity was too great for you to break through your false consciousness without my help—"

"Whoa! That was only the first breakthrough! Look at what happened to me when I consulted you through the medium for my novel *Healing with Padre Pio*—you slew my spiritual vanity with such devastation that it broke the psychic hold that the New Age Religion that I lived for over thirty years had upon me; but I didn't make the connection until now that it might be your voice that asked me *why do you lie?* Were you with me even back then, years before we met through the psychic medium in Barrie, Ontario?"

"Yes. I was always there, in the background, hoping and praying that you would make your way to me when you were ready."

"For what purpose? I know you told me that I came back into my same life to achieve a different outcome because I failed to achieve my goal the first time I lived my life as Orest Stocco, so were you with me to help me achieve what I came to achieve, which was what? To break free of my shadow self? To break free of my unconscious vanity that I brought with me as karmic baggage from one lifetime to the next? Was this why you chose to help me?"

"We agreed to help each other. On the other side you decided that you would like to return to your same life again to see if you could break free of the karmic pattern that you were stuck in. You tried to break free in your immediate past lifetime as Daniel, 'the Aristocratic Trapper,' as you were called in the new land of the Americas when you fled the aristocratic trappings of London, England; but as hard as you tried, you needed help. That's why I asked you the question, why do you lie?"

"God, what that question did to me! I couldn't get it out of my mind. I never thought I was so false and inauthentic until you asked me that question! For the first time in my life I saw myself outside myself, and I hated what I was! And I spent every waking hour redeeming myself from my false self until I finally broke the hold it had upon me that night in the Nipigon Inn Hotel when I was waiting on tables. But I don't want to talk about that now because I've written about this already; what I want to know now is this: where do I go from here?"

"The journey of the self never ends, my friend. I'm on my own journey still, despite all the progress that I have made in my own path to God. And that's the joy of it. You have yet to see that God's love for us is infinite and never ending, and until you do you will always wonder about the journey of the self. But this is the divine mystery. This is why I keep stressing that NOW *is the reality, not tomorrow or the next day.* NOW IS FOREVER.*"*

"I got the feeling you wanted to end your sentence with the word *'capisce.'* I would have. But you are much too kind to be so cheeky. Thank you for that. Yes, I know what you're trying to tell me; but making the shift into NOW is not so easy."

"True. But it's a goal to strive for."

"And I achieve that goal by DOING, right?"

"Yes. In the doing, you are; and in being what you are, you anchor yourself in the NOW. *This is the process. There is still much mystery in the act of doing that you have yet to discover, and you can only do that by mastering the art of doing."*

"I think you're referring to my creative writing, are you not? Because creative writing has become my path, as my last spiritual musing *'Horizontal & Vertical Literature'* brought home to me this week; so by immersing myself in the doing of creative writing, I will discover the divine secret of the NOW of life?"

"Yes."

"And then I can shout, *'O death, where is thy sting? O grave, where is thy victory?'"*

"Well said. But you must quote the entire passage from St. Paul's Corinthians to give it proper context, and then we can discuss it further."

"Give me a moment to look it up…Okay, I found it. It's taken from St. Paul's First Epistle to the Corinthians, Chapter 15: 53-58: *'For the corruptible must put on incorruption, and this mortal must put on immortality. So when this corruptible shall have put on incorruption, and this mortal shall have put on immortality, then shall be brought to pass the saying that is written, Death is swallowed up in victory. O death, where is thy sting? O grave, where is thy victory? The sting of death is sin; and the strength of sin is the law. But thanks be to God, which giveth us the victory through our Lord Jesus Christ. Therefore, my beloved brethren, be ye steadfast, unmovable, always abounding in the work of the Lord, for as much as ye know that your labor is not in vain in the Lord."* That's the whole passage, but I think we should put this into a modern context for today's seeker, don't you?"

"It saddens me to say so, but you are right; the modern seeker does not want to drink in that tired old wine of Christian dogma. But Jesus anticipated this, did he not?"

"Yes, when he said that we cannot pour new wine into old bottles; so, this new wine that we're talking about then is the concept of DOING?"

"Essentially, yes; but that is a wide concept. Doing is the dynamic of the process. It's in how one does what he does that determines the nature and quality of the new wine. This was my purpose in asking you the question, why do you lie? By catching yourself in your false nature, you were compelled to redeem yourself from your falseness; and in the act of self-redemption you discovered the power of the secret way. This is how you transcended yourself and gave birth to your spiritual self in your mother's kitchen that day. So why don't we leave the dynamic of DOING for another time. We've said enough for today."

"You want to leave my reader hanging, don't you?"

"How else can we keep them reading?"

"*Touché*, Padre…"

11. THE STORY OF OUR BECOMING

*"Such is the nature of the human spirit.
It can never be boxed in..."*

    I shouldn't be, but I continue to be surprised by the guiding principle of synchronicity that intercedes in our life to bring our *inner* and the *outer* journey into harmony; but I have to explain what I mean by this, or I will only bring confusion to my story. Before I do however, let me consult my Oracle just to see where this is going…

    "Padre, I got the entry point that I needed for this chapter in the divinely inspired synchronicity that came to me as I was reading *The Path of Initiation, An Introduction to the Life and Thought of Karlfried Graf Durckheim*, by Alphonse Goettmann, which I will disclose later; but first I want to open up a discussion with you on the subject of our becoming. I want to introduce the stages of our evolution through life, but I fear it will sound like speculative thinking which I know it's not because it was my experience. What am I to do?"

    "What is the point that you want to make?"

    "I want to address the continuance of life. Death is just a stage in the long evolution of life, a doorway to another dimension where soul gets a chance to regroup and script the next act of its drama on the stage of life. The point I want to make is that our soul comes from the Body of God and is encoded with God's DNA to return to the Body of God, but it has to go through life to realize its divine nature; this is what I mean by the story of our becoming."

    "Then you must tell the story of your past-life regression to the Body of God and your first primordial human lifetime. Your story may be difficult to believe, but it will be a great relief to many who read it. You have a unique vantage point, and you must share it to give meaning to man's existence. Man cannot fathom the mystery. Your story may help."

"I'm not so sure that anyone wants to know the mystery. I stopped posting my spiritual musings on my blog because it finally dawned on me that my spiritual point of view threatens my readers, and I decided to continue my blog next September with some poetry and short stories instead. I think this will be a better format to tell the story of our becoming, because poetry and stories don't threaten the reader. They may be difficult to understand, as poetry can be, but literature makes different demands upon a reader's sensibilities."

"You're right. Literature can be much more effective, and it would be good for you to exercise your creative muscles by writing poetry and short stories. But your spiritual musings touched a lot of people. You may have stopped writing them, but your spiritual musing books will be read long after you have passed on. They are a big part of your literary legacy."

"Well, I just thought that they had served their purpose and it was time to move on; and in all honesty, it felt good to stop writing and posting them on my blog. I can't explain it, but it felt like a coiled spring had sprung and I had no more anxiety. Was it possible that I was feeling the moral demands that my spiritual musings were asking of my readers?"

"You do make me smile, my friend. Yes, you have given your readers a break from the moral demands your spiritual musings asked of them; and the relief you felt was their relief as much as your relief of the demands that your musings asked of you in writing them."

"And this book on death being the final frontier of life, don't you think this will make demands on my reader? Won't he or she not even want to bother?"

"Never underestimate people. They will continue to surprise you. Such is the nature of the human spirit. It can never be boxed in. Just write your story and let God do the rest. As I used to tell my penitents, live your life to the best of your ability and trust God to take care of you. We are all in God's hands, anyway; so why not acknowledge it?"

"Yes, well; God for many people may very well be a nebulous concept and they won't even give a second glance at books like this. But then, that's what the stages of evolution are all about—from the material-minded to the spiritual sublime. Okay, Padre; I should get to the point of our becoming, because I fear we may be digressing."

DEATH, THE FINAL FRONTIER

"All roads lead to Rome eventually."

"I know, but some are more direct than others. I fear that our forays may be a tad too esoteric for many to follow. But then, what do I know?"

"Do what you must..."

All roads lead to Rome eventually, said my Oracle; which gives credence to the Sufi saying that there are as many ways to God as there are souls. Alphonse Goettmann explores K. G. Durckheim's way to God in his book *The Path of Initiation,* which addresses the question of self-initiation into the mystery of our becoming—what Jesus referred to in one of his sayings when he said that our kingdom would come when we make the two into one; meaning, our inner and outer self. Here's how K. G. Durckheim expressed it:

"Only this union of the existential self with the essential self, dealing with the whole of man, carries him to his full maturity and bears fruits, the first and most important of which is to be able to say "I am" in the full meaning of the word. From this becoming of the "I am" and its full blossoming depends the relationship between man and the world, man and himself, man and Transcendence. At the beginning and at the end, at the origin and in the development of all life is found this transcendent "I am." At the heart of all that is, man secretly senses this great "I Am" from which comes and to which returns all of life. ***Each being is called to realize in his own way this divine "I am" which seeks to express itself in modalities as varied and diverse as are all creatures of the universe***" (*The Path of Initiation*, by Alphonse Goettmann, pp. 36-7, Bold italics mine).

I couldn't believe my eyes. The synchronicity of finding confirmation for my past-life regression to the Body of God and my first primordial human lifetime where I gave birth to the "I am" principle of my own divine nature in Durckheim's own initiation experience was too much for me, and I could not continue writing this chapter on the story of our becoming until I had processed what Durckheim had just revealed; but now, several weeks later, I'm ready to explain the incredible story of our becoming from the perspective of my own initiation into the divine mystery of life's purpose; but I will do so in the following chapter, after first consulting with my Oracle to balance out my energies…

"Padre, now that I got confirmation from K. G. Durckheim that the I Am principle of life is the individuating consciousness of God—or, to be more precise, as far as I can be precise that is, the I Am principle of life is both the potential and realized consciousness of God—I want to ask you if this dialectical exercise that I've embarked upon with this book on death is going where I think it's going. Can you please confirm my intuition?"

"For your reader's sake, please explain where you think this book is going? You must be precise in your answer, because for your reader to understand what you mean by death being the final frontier of life, you must set their feet upon a firm understanding."

"I think this book is pointing to the secret way of life, which is the I Am principle of God that Jesus spoke about in his teaching and which every initiate of the secret way, like K. G. Durckheim and myself, have found and lived by to realize our true nature; which means— and I'm sorry to say this because it may be disconcerting to my reader—that my thoughts on the final frontier of life have opened the door to the alchemical mystery of spiritual self-realization consciousness that my hero Carl Jung spent his life trying to decipher and which he expounded upon in his magnum opus *Mysterium Coniunctionus*. This is what Jesus referred to as the kingdom of heaven. But I fear this may be too much for my reader and will only vex them like my last book *Gurdjieff Was Wrong but His Teaching Works,* and I don't really know what to do about it. Any suggestions?"

"I'm surprised it took you this long to realize it. Yes, this book on death is headed in the direction that you have intuited; but we should explain what that direction is so your reader wont' be left hanging. Let me offer my explanation first, and then you can explain what you mean from your own point of view."

"Fair enough. So what direction are we headed in, then?"
"By way of analogy, what is the goal of the acorn seed?"
"To become an oak tree."

"As is the goal of any seed to become what it is meant to be. What then is man's goal? For what purpose was he born? Can you tell me that?"

"As simple but unbelievable as this may sound, my own journey through life has led me to believe that man's goal in life is to give birth to a new I of God. The universe is the womb of God, and its purpose in the Divine Plan of God is to give birth to God by way of the individuation of the Consciousness of God through man. Can you confirm this perspective?"

"In principle, yes. Man is not realized until he gives birth to his spiritual self. Only then can man be what he has been born to become. Spiritual self-realization consciousness is the blossom of man's existence; that's what drives man to become what he is meant to be, and not until he realizes his goal will he satisfy the longing in his soul."

"And now we come to the crunch: how does man accomplish this goal? That's the mystery and purpose of this book. Man longs to be what he is driven to become, but he doesn't know how to satisfy this longing in his soul; and this is where the story of our becoming as I have experienced it may shed some light upon this mystery. So, should I just move on to my next chapter and introduce the reader to how I initiated myself into the sacred mystery?"

"Your reader cannot wait to turn the page…"

12. THE MYSTERY

"Each soul is its own way into the mystery..."

I just can't jump into the mystery. It would be like asking my reader to dive into the deep end of the pool before they have overcome their fear of drowning; so I'm going to consult my Oracle to help take the fear out of the mystery…

"I hope you won't mind, Padre; but I'd like to open up a dialogue on the question of self-initiation into the secret way of life, because I fear my reader will drown if they're not ready to dive into the deep end of the pool of life."

"You're right to introduce your reader gently into the mystery. Like every child that has to build up its confidence to dive into the deep end of the pool, so does every person have to have the confidence to explore the deepest mystery of man's existence; so, if you don't mind, let me provide an entry into our dialogue on the secret way of life—"

"By all means!"

"This may come as a surprise to you, but the biggest mystery of my life when I was a young friar in San Giovanni Rotondo, was sin. Sin was the preoccupying mystery of my life, and though I had been given the power to absolve my penitents of their sins through the forgiving mercy of our Lord Jesus, I was puzzled by the very nature of sin; and it took many years before I came to see that sin was man's way to salvation. It came to me one day after fourteen hours in the confessional that without sin man could not grow into perfection, because sin was the experience that man needed to see his divine nature; and not until I grasped the mystery of sin did I understand the reason for man's existence."

"Believe it or not, I think I know where you're going with this."

"That doesn't surprise me. After all, you have transitioned beautifully from the Information Age to the Age of Intuition, as the

author of the books that you are reading has expressed the emerging new species of man—what your friend Teresa called 'Homo nuovo' in her book Living Beyond the Five Senses. *But we can talk about this later. The point we have to make clear in this dialogue is that there are as many pathways into the secret way of life as there are souls in the world, because each soul is its own way into the mystery. Perhaps you can explain this for your reader."*

"I think you did it best with your epiphany on sin. Do you remember when I confronted you on the issue of sin in one of my spiritual healing sessions with the psychic medium who channeled you? Good God, I was bold with you; wasn't I?"

"You were. And I welcomed the opportunity to affirm your insight on sin. You were perfectly correct to say that there really is no such thing as sin, only human experience; and that was my epiphany that day in the confessional. It simply came to me that sin was man's pathway to his divine nature and not the folly we believed sin to be; and once I realized this my whole attitude on sin changed. I no longer judged man for his sin, because I understood sin to be his experience into the mystery. This was a revelation to me, and it still gives me goosebumps thinking about my experience that day. It changed my life forever."

"Okay; let's explore this, then. But I have to tell you first, Padre; this is not the entry point that I expected for our dialogue on the secret way of life. You've taken me by surprise, as you did a number of times when I had my spiritual healing sessions with you. You revealed things to me that I would never have expected, and to tell me now that you had an epiphany on sin while you were listening to your penitents in the confessional opens up a whole new perspective on man's spiritual indiscretions—if I may be allowed to describe sin this way. After all, every spiritual teaching throughout history has given man moral guidelines to avoid behavior that deviates from the path to salvation; but salvation, as we have come to realize today is not heaven, but realizing our own divine nature. Which brings us back to the mystery of the secret way. If I understand you correctly, you came to see sin as a human experience that concentrated man's awareness to help him realize that he is more than a human body. He is a perfect soul, and sin is man's way of coming to the realization of his divine nature. Have I got the gist of your premise?"

"There are two ways that man experiences life. Man can have a positive experience with life, and a negative experience with life. A positive experience nourishes soul directly, and a negative experience nourishes soul indirectly. When man sins, he has a negative experience with life; and the energy that man realizes from a negative experience has to be transformed to nourish his soul. Unless man takes the initiative and transforms his negative experiences by redressing them with positive experiences, he suffers; but all is not lost, because in God's Divine Plan man is never forsaken. Suffering is life's way of transmuting man's negative energy into positive energy. This is the alchemical mystery of the secret way of life, which the Gnostics and later the mystical alchemists exploited through their teachings and which you discovered while living Gurdjieff's system of self-transformation. Suffering transforms man's negative energy and nourishes man's soul; and the more man grows in his spiritual body, the more he awakens to his divine nature. This was my epiphany in the confessional that day, and it gives me great pleasure to share this with you this morning."

"This is what the alchemists meant by transmuting lead into gold, isn't it?"

"Yes. They discovered the mystical science of self-transformation. They took the concentrated lode of human experience and transmuted it into spiritual gold to nourish Homo nuovo. This is the core mystery of the secret way of life. If you would, please explain this for your reader who has not quite grasped the gist of what we're talking about."

"I'd love to, because this will be a wonderful entry into my regression experience that initiated me into the mystery. If I may, then; let me refer to my one true hero, Carl Gustav Jung—and I call him my one true hero because he's the only person that I have become acquainted with, albeit through his writing (except for my dream experience with him), who had the courage to go where his *daemon* demanded him to go, right to the source of his being, which he goes to great lengths to explain with his *psychology of individuation*. Jung's whole psychology rests upon the premise that the psyche is innately teleological, forever in pursuit of a future goal, and this goal is the realization of a self. I have not yet come across anyone else who has given expression to the teleological purpose of man's existence as clearly as Jung has expressed it in his *psychology of individuation*. Perhaps the Persian poet Rumi, who speaks of the mystery of man's becoming in the mystical language of poetry; but because his poetry is so puzzling one has difficulty grasping the essential mystery of the secret way, which I hope to make clear with my past-life regression experience to the Body of God and my first primordial human lifetime. So, if I may Padre; do you think this would be the right time to share my experience of how I was initiated into the divine mystery, and then I can expound upon the secret way of self-transformation through life experience?"

"I do; but I would suggest you explain the whole experience. Not in the detail that you employed in your novel Cathedral of My Past Lives, *but in enough detail to let your reader see that it was a goal of yours to write a book on your own past lives. Perhaps you can devote a whole chapter to your initiation experience?"*

"Good idea. Do you have a chapter title for me also?"

"Just give it to your creative self, why don't you?"

"And so I shall…"

13. MY REGRESSION TO THE BODY OF GOD

*"We are all atoms of God's Body
divinely encoded to realize God's nature…"*

It's unfortunate that C. G. Jung didn't embrace what Socrates called "a doctrine uttered in secret," by which he meant the teaching of reincarnation; but Jung had good reason not to, because if he had it would have damaged his scientific credibility, and he had his hands full as it was establishing his personal psychology for the modern world.

So it wasn't that he didn't believe in reincarnation, which he comes very close to admitting in his memoir *Memories, Dreams, Reflections*; he simply focused on the psyche, which was enough to keep him busy his entire professional life.

Ironically however, as Jesus pointed out to the artist Glenda Green who painted his portrait and recorded her experience in *Love without End, Jesus Speaks,* one's present lifetime is always the medium for accomplishing one's teleological purpose of realizing one's true self, which would render reincarnation moot. As Jesus expressed it to Glenda Green while she painted his portrait: `There is no other place to find yourself.` **Now** *is your only context."* Here's what Jesus said about reincarnation:

"The philosophy of reincarnation is not that simple. It does affirm your continuity, and that is good. However, there's a twist in it which defers your immortality back to structure and linearity, which is not true. Your immortality is not imprisoned within a wheel of life, or pathway of cause and effect. Neither are you the product of linear evolvement. **_You were created in perfection, and perfect love, and you do continue to re-manifest infinitely, but according to the will of the Father, and according to your own purposes, your own love, and your own place of service and learning._** You actually only live one life! It's just a very long one, with many chapters" (*Love without End,*

DEATH, THE FINAL FRONTIER

Jesus Speaks, by Glenda Green, pp. 76-77, Bold italics and underscoring mine).

What Jesus said about reincarnation resonated with me, but only because I had worked out the divine mystery of reincarnation as I wrote my autobiographical novel *Cathedral of My Past Lives* that was based upon my seven past-life regressions; but it behooves me to explain why I had my regressions before I relate the miraculous experience that put this whole issue of reincarnation into proper perspective for me.

Despite my Roman Catholic faith growing up, when I encountered the "doctrine uttered in secret" I felt an immediate attraction to it; and though it threw my Christian faith into confusion, I pursued the doctrine of reincarnation. And the more I read on reincarnation, the more convinced I was that when we die we come back to live life over again; and my concern then became—*why do we come back to live life over again?*

Aside from having to deal with why my Roman Catholic faith refuted the existence of reincarnation, I was plagued by an obsessive desire (one could call it pathological) to find my true self; but I've expounded upon this in my book *The Summoning of Noman*, so I need not repeat myself here. Suffice to say that I was *driven* to find an answer to the question that catapulted me into my spiritual quest—**who am I?**

My quest to find an answer to this question led me to Gurdjieff's teaching of *conscious effort* and *intentional suffering,* which awakened me to the secret way in Christ's sayings and parables; and as I lived the secret way I got the answer to my question one summer day in my mother's kitchen while she was kneading bread dough on the kitchen table.

As my mother and I were talking, I had a subtle shift in self-consciousness from my existential self to my essential self and awakened to my immortal nature, and I *knew* that the infinite "I Am" consciousness of God and my I-am consciousness were one and the same I. In a fraction of a second I gave birth to my spiritual nature, and I knew that I was *me*, my immortal self; and although this satisfied the longing in my soul to know *who I was*, I still longed to know *why I was* and where I came from; and this is what my seven past-life regressions answered for me when Penny and I moved to Georgian Bay many years later.

The merciful law of divine synchronicity made it happen: I met a woman at a spiritual function in Orillia, Ontario—the hometown of Stephen Leacock, whose book *Sunset Sketches of a Little Town* gave me much laughter; and in the course of our conversation she told me that she practiced Reiki and also did past-life regressions, and she gave me her card.

But before I get to my past-life regression that initiated me into the mystery of our destined purpose in life, let me say a word or two about synchronicity—something that I'm exploring more deeply in my work-in-progress *The Merciful Law of Divine Synchronicity* which I put on hold to explore the final frontier of life with this story. It didn't come to me in one glorious epiphany, it happened over time; with every little coincidence and synchronicity that I experienced in the course of my life, I became a little more aware of what I eventually came to call *"the omniscient guiding principle of life."* This guiding principle is Divine Spirit, though it has been called by many names; and I came to see that when we're ready to move onto the next stage of our journey to what Jung called "wholeness and completeness," the merciful guiding principle of life kicks in, and we are blessed with a synchronicity experience that can change our life—like meeting the lady at our spiritual function in Orillia who just happened to do past-life regressions.

Obviously, I was ready to explore this new pathway which would open me up to whole new dimensions of my life or I would not have met this woman; and, believe me, the circumstances that led to this life-changing synchronicity were so traumatizing that I will only be able to do them justice in a novel, which I hope to write one day. The point I want to make is that **synchronicity only happens when one is ready for a larger perspective on life**, and I was ready; so I made arrangements with this lady and had seven past-life regressions, one per month for seven months. (I was supposed to have ten, but seven were enough.)

Just to be clear, then; synchronicity happened because I wanted to have my own past-life regressions ever since I read Jess Stearn's book on Taylor Caldwell's past lives, but because new pathways of self-discovery only open up to us when we're ready I had to wait years before I was ready for my regressions; that's why I said that I must have been ready or I would not have met my regressionist in Orillia when Penny and I moved from my hometown to Tiny Beaches, Georgian Bay. In my fourth regression I experienced myself in the Body of God where all souls come from, and in the same regression I went back to my first primordial human lifetime as the alpha male of a small group of higher primates and I gave birth to a new "I" of God; or, to be less dramatic, I experienced the dawning of my own reflective self-consciousness, proving (for myself at least) the origin of our reflective self.

When I had this regression, I had no idea why I was blessed to experience myself first in the Body of God as a group soul; that is, as an embryonic soul with no reflective self-consciousness, and then experienced myself in my first primordial human lifetime as a higher primate when I had the dawning of my own reflective self-consciousness, and it took a long time to work this out as I wrote my novel *Cathedral of My Past Lives*. And now that I have the answer to this miraculous twin-experience in my fourth past-life regression, I can put some meat on what Jesus said: **"You were created in perfection, and perfect love, and you do continue to re-manifest infinitely, but according to the will of the Father, and according to your own purposes, your own love, and your own place of service and learning."**

In my regression, I experienced myself as an embryonic soul—perfectly happy in my blissful state of group consciousness in the Body of God, which I experienced as an infinite ocean of love and mercy; but I had no reflective self-consciousness. I know this, because I was witnessing myself from my evolved state of self-consciousness; and then for reasons which only became clear to me much later as I was working on *Cathedral of My Past Lives, the omniscient guiding principle of life* blessed me with the experience of my first primordial human lifetime when I gave birth to my reflective self-consciousness. And as I eventually worked out in my writing, the reason I was allowed to have this dual experience was because it was given to me to work out the paradox of man's free will within the context of God's Will, which took me many years to resolve to my complete satisfaction.

Jesus calls God's Will *"the will of the Father,"* and man's free will he defines as *"your own purposes, your own love, and your own place of service and learning."* And given my dual experience of being an un-self-realized soul that gave birth to its own reflective self-consciousness, I finally resolved the mystery of why we keep coming back to live life over again life after life after life—because **we are all atoms of God's Body divinely encoded to realize God's nature through the evolution of our own reflective self-consciousness;** and not until we give birth to our spiritual self, which Jesus taught us how to do with the secret way that he couched in his sayings and parables, will we be whole and complete.

In effect, every soul is an atom of God encoded to realize its divine nature (**the will of the Father**), but we can only do this according to **our own purposes, our own love, and our own place of service and learning**—meaning, through our own karmic destiny which we create ourselves by the choices we make in life; and the only way we can do this—*as I painfully came to learn through my other past-life regressions that informed me of the karmic baggage that I brought with me from one lifetime to the next!* —is by mastering the art of aligning our free will with the Will of our Father, which is what I learned how to do with Gurdjieff's teaching of *conscious effort* and *intentional suffering* and by putting to practice the teachings of the secret way that Jesus couched in his sayings and parable.

"Well, Padre; did I do my experience justice, or was it too much for the reader?"

"It would have been too much had you not provided a credible context with Jesus Christ's description of reincarnation that he shared with the artist who painted his portrait, which I'm sure many of your readers will follow up on by reading Glenda Green's book Love without End, Jesus Speaks—"

"Pardon my interruption, but if I haven't mentioned this already it was you who recommended this book to the psychic medium who channeled you for my spiritual healing sessions, which I went out and picked up that same day at a friend's used bookstore in Barrie, plus Glenda's follow-up book *The Keys of Jeshua*; so, thank you Padre."

DEATH, THE FINAL FRONTIER

"You're welcome. Now, back to your regression to the Body of God and to your first primordial human lifetime where you experienced the dawning of your reflective self-consciousness, let me mention that this is one way for the spark of God to individuate through life. There are others. But it would not be appropriate for this book to discuss other paths for soul's evolution through life. That's for others to do. Your calling is to write about your own journey to wholeness, and this book brings much clarity to the individuation of the I of God through natural evolution. Nature evolves man so far, and then man must take evolution into his own hands, and this is what you did. So, yes I am very pleased with how you brought credibility to your incredible experience within the context of Christ's teaching."

"But bear in mind that I want to demystify this whole process of our becoming, which is why I have included Jung's psychology of individuation in my context. I don't want to give the impression that I'm on some kind of spiritual mission here. I couldn't care less how people live their life. All I want to do is bring some clarity to the human condition, which every writer wants to do. I have a story to tell, and I'm telling it according to my calling."

"Don't get excited. I know you're still smarting from your experience with that New Age Religion, but it gave you what you needed to break free of your unconscious vanity; so be thankful for the experience and move on to new horizons."

"I won't be free to move on until I write about my experience. I got rid of some of my anger with my book *The Pearl of Great Price*, but I have to write another book to get rid of the rest of my anger at that teaching's deceptive history and purloined wisdom. So, sorry Padre; I can't move on just yet. I have to pour all of that good anger energy into another story, which I hope to write this coming winter. My working title is 'The Funeral Service'."

"You do like to grind your axes, don't you?"

"That's where our best novels come from, don't they?"

"Admittedly so, my friend. But at least you are conscious of your anger, which should make for an interesting story. Most writers aren't conscious of their anger. They just write to get rid of it. That's how they resolve their shadow side. But we're off topic."

"I know. Okay, thank you for the chat. I think I heard my next chapter calling me in what you said about writers writing to resolve their shadow side…I think I heard Leo Tolstoy calling me…*The Death of Ivan Ilych*…thank you for the inspiration, Padre."

"You're welcome…"

14. THE IVAN ILYCH PROBLEM

"Literature is the lifeblood of human experience..."

"When I am not, what will be there? There will be nothing. Then where shall I be when I am no more? Can this be dying?" said Ivan Ilych in Tolstoy's novella "The Death of Ivan Ilych," the story of one man's reflections upon his life as he approaches his final hour; and like Ivan Ilych, we all wonder if when we die we are no more.

Late in his life Leo Tolstoy asked the fateful question: "Is there any meaning to our life that is not destroyed by death?" I answered this question with my novel *What Would I Say Today If I Were to Die Tomorrow?* I put myself under the fabled Sword of Damocles and lived my life as though today would be my last, which gave me the courage to write my final thoughts, as it were; and as far removed in time as my novel may be from Tolstoy's "The Death of Ivan Ilych," I know that *What Would I Say Today If I Were to Die Tomorrow?* would be a promising answer to Ivan Ilych's haunting questions about death; but I wonder what my Oracle has to say about the Ivan Ilych problem...

"I hope you don't mind, Padre; but I'm in a bit of a quandary, given that the Ivan Ilych problem is no more resolved today than when Tolstoy tackled it in "The Death of Ivan Ilych" which was published in 1886, a hundred and thirty years ago, and by this I mean man's haunting doubt about the purpose of life—and, of course, if death is the final curtain. Are you up to discussing this today?"

"This is central to your book. Yes, of course I would love to discuss it with you. What specifically are you asking?"

"It takes Ivan Ilych a long time to realize that his life is a lie, which is why he goes back to the innocence of his childhood when he was natural, spontaneous, and free to be himself; and that's what I tried to point out in *What Would I Say Today If I Were to Die Tomorrow?* I wanted to illustrate that our life-lie keeps us from experiencing our essential self. As K. G. Durckheim expressed it, man gets stuck in his existential self and loses contact with his essential self. Ivan Ilych lost contact with his essential self and could not make sense of life from the perspective of his mortal existential nature. Specifically, then; I want to know what you think one should do to reconnect with his immortal essential self so that he won't be faced with what I've come to see as the Ivan Ilych problem."

"I like the way you framed Tolstoy's moral dilemma. I had to deal with man's fear of death every day in the confessional, and it never failed to move me how death could have so much power over man; and my only consolation at the time was to encourage my penitents to believe in Christ's redemptive power and a heavenly afterlife. That was then, and I do not subtract from that equation. But from my perspective over here I can offer you a much wider understanding, and what I would say about the Ivan Ilych problem is that man cannot escape the dual consciousness of his nature. Man is made of matter and Spirit, and the consciousness of one is mortal and the other immortal. That's man's dilemma, and the solution to the Ivan Ilych problem—"

"Sorry for the interruption, Padre; but you're not telling me anything new. Durckheim and countless others have figured this out, but little has changed to solve Ivan's Ilych's dilemma. Or are you suggesting—*which I think you are!* — that this is simply the human condition, and that it's up to us to figure it out for ourselves?"

"And I was accused of being blunt? Yes, you are correct. We are responsible for our own spiritual awakening. But unfortunately, man needs help. As your own mentor expressed it, nature will only evolve man so far and no further. To complete the journey to wholeness and completeness, man needs incentive. This is provided by what you have so aptly described as 'the omniscient guiding principle of life.' So man is not alone in his dilemma. He is always given help when he needs it. It's up to man to take it or not. No one—and I mean no one! — is ever left stranded in the minefields of life."

"If I didn't believe in reincarnation, I'd argue the point with you; but I do, so I know that we are always given another opportunity to resolve our dilemma. But Tolstoy didn't go that far. He was stuck in the Christian paradigm. We know different, and this is the perspective I'd like to offer. Death is not the end, as Ivan Ilych feared.

DEATH, THE FINAL FRONTIER

It's a door to a new beginning; but how can one possibly weave this perspective into the tapestry of contemporary literature?"

"*That's your challenge, my friend.*"

"And so it is. But this intrigues me. I've already solved the riddle of why people are so slow to believe in reincarnation, so my problem is not proving it; it's waking readers up to the reality of their destined purpose. I tried with my spiritual musings blog, but my musings stretched logic too far for the reader and became threatening. This is why I turned to writing literature—poetry, short stories, and novels. Literature has a way of distilling life to its essential purpose, and out of this we draw meaning to the human condition. To put it differently, literature tries to make order out of the chaos of life. That's what I hope to do with my creative writing. I want to take my own experience when I write and transform it into a deeper perception of that experience with the transformative power of my imagination, which I believe won't be so threatening to the reader. If I may, I've already written 73 poems for my book of poetry (*Not My Circus, Not My Monkeys)*, and I'd like to share the poem I wrote this morning, because it speaks to the aesthetic power of literature: —

Lifeblood

When I want inspiration
I turn to literature,
the lifeblood of human
experience.

Not music, nature, religion,
or—God forbid! another
elusive muse; just the lifeblood
of human experience.

Varied, mundane or complex,
poem, prose, essay, each written
in the lifeblood of human
experience.

Experience is the teacher,

guide, and lesson all rolled up
into one, the numinous spirit
of implacable wisdom, —

My inspiration!

    "When Picasso said it took his whole life to learn how to paint like a child, I can also say that it took my whole life to learn how to see un-blinkered like a child; that's the premise of this poem—to discard all we are taught to believe and trust human experience to give us the truth we need to make our way through life. This is the value of literature."

    "Well said. By all means, with my blessings continue writing poetry. But I cannot wait to read some of your stories, those not written yet. Like The Mountie's Last Case. *You shine best in your stories, something you have yet to realize. But you will."*

    "Sometimes life feels like Chinese water torture, one terrifying drop at a time; that's how slow we are to absorb life's implacable wisdom. So what's the answer, if you don't mind another presumptuous question?"

    "Now is your only context. When you fix this in your mind, you eliminate the fear of dying and solve the Ivan Ilych problem. Every moment is an entry into the kingdom of your essential self. This is what you see in literature. Don't worry about tomorrow. Write today and let tomorrow unfold accordingly. This is enough for now."

    "On to the Ivan Ilych problem, then…"

15. SOLVING THE IVAN ILYCH PROBLEM

"Literature is not enough. Neither is art, religion, science, philosophy, psychology, or any discipline..."

Ivan Ilych is everywhere. He is Everyman. He could be your next door neighbor, a man so postured he can't tell the lie of his life from the truth of his life, and he too fears dying like Ivan Ilych.

This is the curious thing about human nature. It was so during the time of Tolstoy and long before him, and it is still so today because of the dual consciousness of our nature. But it's next to impossible to explain the consciousness of our dual nature. I've done so to my own satisfaction—*which took most of my adult life to do!* —but how can I apply this to the Ivan Ilych problem without taxing my reader's credulity? Do you know, Padre?

"I didn't expect to be consulted so soon. But that's fine. We can discuss the dual nature of man. This is the premise upon which Christ founded his teaching of salvation. This is what the ancients called 'sacred knowledge.' But the psychology of man has evolved enough to offer a conceptual understanding of man's dual nature. Doctor Jung gives us a good picture with his psychology of individuation. Why don't we start from there?"

"Gladly. But I have to ask you something first. I think Carl Jung is still a good fifty years ahead of his time with respect to his understanding of the sacred knowledge. He initiated himself into the secret way of life, which he identified as the 'individuation process,' but society has not grasped the essential principle of his psychology, which is the individuation of the inherent self of the human psyche. Am I correct in this?"

"Basically, yes. He was an initiate of the secret way, which he reveals in the experience he had with his own unconscious that he recorded in The Red Book, *but only a few people have caught the divine imperative of his teaching. You have. This is why you admire him so much, because he confirms your own individuation process. So*

perhaps you can couch the Ivan Ilych problem in Jungian terminology. In psychological concepts, that is."

"I can try. Simply put, Ivan Ilych is stuck in his shadow self. The shadow is a Jungian concept which describes the repressed dark side of our ego personality. This is many people's problem. They are so shadow-afflicted that they can no longer tell the lie from the truth of their life and have become their own fool. If I may, I'd like to quote a poem inspired by a man which speaks to the Ivan Ilych problem. Would you like to hear it?"

"By all means. Anything to shed light upon the Ivan Ilych problem."

"Alright. Here's my freshly-minted poem—

Peach Cobbler

He walked over with his drink of rye,
returning the tea towel Penny had used
to carry over her warm peach cobbler
the other day, and sat down with me in
the shade of the maple tree where I was
reading the Freud/Jung letters to satisfy
my curiosity on the private relationship
of the founding fathers of psychotherapy,
my preference by far for Jung who became
my hero of the *secret way* that he brought
into the open with his gnostic *psychology
of individuation,* and taking a gulp of rye,
idiosyncratic to annoyance, preferential
eater and scoffer of all foods foreign to
his palate (how would he know if he does
not try them?), proceeded to offer his
opinion on Jung's painful break with his
mentor, uninformed and fatuous, and I
inquired about Penny's cobbler, expecting
him to be polite whether he liked it or not;
but he chose not to lie and told me it was
too sweet for his liking, egregious cognitive
dissonance for a man whose whole life was

a lie, but that's how the shadow plays,
always dancing to the tune of self-serving logic in
the hope of finding a partner to dance with.
"Oh well," said I, smiling at his little game;
"it was a new recipe, and you were the
neighborly guinea pigs."

"This man is stuck in his shadow, but he cannot see his self-deception and suffers all the symptoms of the shadow-afflicted personality like Ivan Ilych—fear, anxiety, and depression. This is what happened to Ernest Hemingway; he was so shadow-afflicted that he lost control of his life with guilt and booze and killed himself. I explored this in *The Lion that Swallowed Hemingway*. Jung plays a big part in this book also, because he was the opposite of my high school hero. Jung shifted his center of gravity to his essential self and became a master of the sacred knowledge. He's been called a mystic, but that's only because he penetrated the secret of the life process. I've also written about this in *Gurdjieff Was Wrong but His Teaching Works,* but these two books have rubbed readers the wrong way and got nasty reviews on Amazon; so what's a person to do, Padre? People don't want to be told that they are slaves of their own shadow, like the man in my poem; that's why they get offended when their shadow is exposed. The shadow is a devilish creature, always making nasty just to feed off the negative energies that it foments with its nastiness; but I'm onto the shadow's logic, and I don't suffer the shadow easily, as my poem would indicate. The tragedy of Ivan Ilych is that he got stuck in his shadow personality; that's why he suffered doubt, anxiety, and depression. He feared his own nothingness, which the shadow is because the shadow is what it is not and not what it is. It's a paradoxical creature, because it's made up of the consciousness of the non-being of our nature; but how can I get the reader to see that our shadow is real in its own way and has power over our ego personality; or our existential self, as K. G. Durckheim would say?"

"There you have it. That's the Ivan Ilych problem in a nutshell."

"It seems that Tolstoy's Ivan Ilych has brought us to the crux of man's existential dilemma, then—the consciousness of our mortality. Is this the final frontier of life, the consciousness of our mortality? Is death the mirror that reflects the mortality of our existential self back to us? And if we are centered in our mortal existential self, won't this terrify us as it did Ivan Ilych? You don't have to answer that, Padre; I know the answer. I've known it for a long time, but I never put it together this way before. My problem as a writer has always been to get the reader to see that the mortal self that he sees in the mirror is his existential self and not his immortal essential self; but that, as I also came to see, is an individual journey of self-discovery. Do you see my dilemma, Padre? As the saying goes, you can lead a horse to water—"

"That's the purpose of literature, isn't it? To lead the reader to the living water of eternal life, as you have just done with your poem 'Peach Cobbler.' After all, what is the distilled truth of life experience if not the living water of eternal life?"

"If by living water of eternal life you mean the secret way of life, I agree; but still, the reader has no idea that the distilled truth of life experience is the living water of the secret way of life. Despite how excited the reader may be by a poem or story, despite how moved they may be emotionally, they still cannot make the connection that what moves them about a poem or story is the inherent wisdom of the secret way of life that is the essential truth of the writer's own experiences that he magnifies in his writing, if you know what I mean?"

"I know exactly what you mean. But your concept may be too abstract for your reader. If you will permit me, a writer writes from his experience. As he writes, he engages his creative imagination, and this transforms the writer's experience. In this transformation, the writer gets to the essential truth of his experience. This truth is the living water of literature that sets one free from one's shadow personality. This is why literature can be so moving to the reader. The essential truth of a poem or story speaks the secret way, as you did in your poem 'Peach Cobbler.' As Jesus would say, the reader drinks in the water of eternal life when they are moved by a poem or story. Literature speaks to them on a soul level. This is why you want to write poetry and stories, because you have finally come to see that the most effective way to get the reader to drink in the water of eternal life is through literature. People don't want to be told how to live

their life. Didn't Emily Dickinson come to this realization? 'Tell the truth, but tell it slant /Success in circuit lies,' she wrote. That's what literature does. It tells the truth slanted for the reader's comfort, as you just did with your poem."

"You also make me smile, Padre! Yes, literature does slant the truth—because the reader is too thick in their own shadow to take the truth directly. Like Jack Nicholson shouted to Tom Cruise in the movie *A Few Good Men,* 'YOU CAN'T HANDLE THE TRUTH!' That's how I feel about the reader. That's what I learned the hard way with my spiritual musings. But you were waiting for me to come to this realization, weren't you? You were waiting for me to wake up to my own arrogance, weren't you? It took four volumes of spiritual musings for me to see the arrogance of my own journey of self-discovery. God, what a fool I was!"

"A magnificent fool, if I may say so. You were noble in your intentions, and this absolves you of your folly. But that part of your journey is over now. Let's concentrate on this book so you can devote your time to writing poetry and stories."

"Do you see the irony, Padre?"

"Of course I do. The reader has to be tricked for his own good. And this is getting very close to the mystery of Christ's crucifixion. Jesus died on the cross because he too saw that he had to tell the truth slanted, because man cannot swallow the hard truth that he is responsible for his own salvation. Jesus had to find a way to give man the knowledge of salvation from the dual consciousness of his own nature without scaring him away from the sacred knowledge, and he did this with his crucifixion which symbolized the death of his lower self, because in the death of the lower self man realizes his higher nature. That's the core message of Christ's teaching and the living water of eternal life in literature. Now do you understand why I could not share this with you when you were working on your novel Healing with Padre Pio? You weren't ready for this knowledge then. Now you are."

"I understand. But let me run this by you, if I may? I may have been arrogant in my spiritual musings, hoping to plow my way into the reader's mind and introduce them to the sacred knowledge of the secret way of life; but the only reason I did that was because I had come to the realization that literature was not enough to wake man up to his dual nature. I wrote about this in several books, specifically in *The Lion that Swallowed Hemingway*. That's why Katherine Mansfield went to Gurdjieff. Literature wasn't enough for her. She needed something more to resolve her inauthentic life. She needed a system of self-transformation. She needed the sacred knowledge of the secret way of life. She came to that realization on her own, but it was too late for her; she died of tuberculosis at the age of thirty-four. So realizing that literature is not enough to get man to wake up to his essential self, then why even bother? That's what I'd like you to answer for me now: why bother writing poems and stories if literature is not enough? Do you see the irony?"

"You do ask the tough questions. But you deserve an answer. You have been totally honest in your efforts to resolve the riddle of life, and you followed every clue that you were given by your guiding principle; so, allow me to answer your question."

"By all means. I can't wait for your answer!"

"You are absolutely correct; literature is not enough. Neither is art, religion, science, philosophy, psychology, or any discipline because the natural way of life can only take one so far on their journey to wholeness and completeness; and then one must take evolution into their own hands. This was your realization, and your dilemma. Once you solved the riddle you sought to share it with your readers, but you finally came to realize with your final spiritual musing 'Horizontal & Vertical Literature' that there was a distinction between literature that speaks the secret way of life and literature that does not, and you brought your literary experiment with your spiritual musings to closure because you could not say anything more about the inherent value of literature. You brought your reader to the realization that literature inspires one to live their own life, and that's the most that literature can do; but to live their life honestly. That's the moral of Tolstoy's story 'The Death of Ivan Ilych.' Tolstoy saw Ivan Ilych's problem, but he couldn't resolve it for him. Neither can any man resolve the Ivan Ilych problem until one becomes aware of it. And this is why you should write literature. Your poems and stories will awaken the reader to their dual nature, as Tolstoy did with Ivan Ilych. Ivan Ilych did not go to his grave blind to his false nature. He finally realized that his life was a lie, and that's the most literature can to for the reader; which is to say, wake the reader up to their dual

nature. *What else can the writer do for the reader? He can't force the reader to be true to himself. Does that answer your question?"*

"On the whole. The problem I had was getting the reader to see that even being true to oneself is not enough to satisfy one's longing for wholeness. Ivan Ilych believed that he was an honest and honorable man, just as my neighbor thinks he is; but which self is he being true to—his existential or essential self? That's what I tried to spell out with my spiritual musings by asking the question 'Can a person be false and still be true?' But I failed to make any headway. I pushed the envelope too far, and I had to stop writing my spiritual musings. So I'm back to where I started: why bother leading the horse to water?"

"But it's not your responsibility if the horse drinks or not, is it?"

"Pardon my laughter, Padre; but wasn't that your problem also? How many times did you scold your penitents for their repeated follies?"

"Don't remind me. Yes, I too suffered from the need to save the world. And it wasn't until late in life that I came to realize that the world is what it is and the most we can do is to help make it a better place. I did my best with what I had to work with. But you're right to find this humorous. Yes, man can be true to himself as Ivan Ilych was; but that didn't take away his fear of dying. He was, as you say, stuck in the consciousness of his false self; but he did go to his grave aware of his false nature, and that's literature's victory."

"This is why I had to introduce the reader to the big picture of God's Divine Plan, because unless one sees that we live more than one lifetime then literature's victory would be hollow. It wouldn't mean a damn thing if Ivan Ilych only lived one lifetime. But because in God's Divine Plan soul has as many lives as it will take to realize its destined purpose, then literature indeed triumphs in its inspiration. So Padre, I guess I got my answer. I have to write poetry and stories to fulfill my own destined purpose, but I do so now in the realization that literature will never be enough to resolve the Ivan Ilych problem, but enough to get the ball rolling; and that's the best that I can do."

"Well said, my friend..."

16. THE GUIDING PRINCIPLE OF LITERATURE

"The daemon is one's creative spirit..."

"One writes out of one thing only—one's own experience," said Richard Wright, the author of *Go Tell It on the Mountain,* in the anthology *The Art of the Short Story* by Dana Gioia and R. S. Gwynn. "Everything depends upon how relentlessly one forces from this experience the last drop, sweet or bitter, it can possibly give. This is the only real concern of the artist, to recreate out of the disorder of life that order which is art," added Wright.

In effect Richard Wright, as all writers, wanted to make sense out of life, to see if life has meaning and purpose, and some writers feel it does and others don't. That was Tolstoy's purpose with "The Death of Ivan Ilych." He wanted Ivan to face his own death to see how it would affect him, and Tolstoy learned that when man envelops his life in a lie he won't be happy; he will be lonely, sad, and miserable like Ivan Ilych.

Happiness then appears to be a circumstance of life, not the teleological purpose; this is why writers keep writing, to explore if life has inherent meaning. Is life a tale told by an idiot full of sound and fury signifying nothing, or is life meaningful and purposive?

I wanted to be a writer from the earliest age. In high school I discovered literature. I was deeply moved by literature. Literature spoke to me. Not to my mind, but to my soul. In some deep and inexplicable way, literature told me something that I needed to know. I couldn't explain what this "something" was, and it would take many years to discover this mysterious *je ne sais quoi* of literature; but when I did, literature made sense to me.

If I may, let me quote a poem I wrote to illustrate the effect literature had on me in high school with a book that I stole from our school library and never returned: —

DEATH, THE FINAL FRONTIER

The Smell of Life

"I love the smell of this book,"
said Penny Lynn this morning.
"It smells of life."

She was reading the book
I stole from high school half
a century ago, *Great Short
Stories from the World's
Literature,* and had only forty
more pages to go.

But I wondered to myself
as I worked on my new book
Death, the Final Frontier,
was it the old musky library
book that smelled of life,
or the stories? —

The Snows of Kilimanjaro
stunk to high heaven of
Hemingway's self-betrayal,
The Wall by Sartre puissant
with the absurdity of life,
and *The Three Hermits* by
Tolstoy redolent with
lingering hope!

  Did I sense in these great short stories from the world's literature that mysterious *je ne sais quoi* that literature seems to possess? That last bitter/sweet drop of life experience? Is this why I was so moved by these stories? Why they spoke to me?

  I believe so. And I believe this is why people are drawn to literature. When I read Somerset Maugham's novel *The Razor's Edge* in grade twelve, I was so moved by Maugham's hero Larry Darrell's heroic quest for the meaning and purpose of life that he ignited a spark in me that was to change my life forever; such is the power of what I can only call "the guiding principle of literature."

Maugham's novel spoke to me. It spoke to me in the mystical language of the soul, a silent guidance that tells one what they need to know. I needed to know that there were seekers who dropped out of life to search for the meaning and purpose of life, which was exactly what I did a few years after high school. I divested myself of my pool hall and vending machine business and went to France to begin my quest for my true self, so I'm intimately familiar with the power of literature. But literature was not enough to resolve my dilemma. I needed *conscious* guidance, which I serendipitously found in Gurdjieff's teaching when I returned from Annecy, France and went to Lakehead University to study philosophy.

I explored all of this in my literary memoir *The Lion that Swallowed Hemingway* and another provocative book *Gurdjieff Was Wrong but His Teaching Works*, so I need not repeat myself here. I simply want to make the point that there is a guiding principle in literature that tells us how to negotiate our way through life; but, as my Oracle and I have discussed, literature is not enough to satisfy the longing in our soul for wholeness and completeness. One needs more than the silent message of literature…

"I think we've come to the point of no return, Padre. There's no turning back now, and I have no choice but to go where my *daemon* takes me to bring this book to fruition; but if you would indulge me, can we talk about this concept of the *daemon*?"

"As you wish. If anyone was ever driven by their daemon, you were; so you have plenty to say on the subject. But bear in mind that the concept of the daemon is much more mysterious than most artists realize. The daemon is one's creative spirit, but this spirit takes many lifetimes to realize itself as the driving force of one's life—"

"The soul's code! Pardon my interruption, Padre; but James Hillman sprang to mind. He was a Jungian analyst who wrote a book called *The Soul's Code, In Search of Character and Calling*, which I read several times because it spoke to my need to understand the power of the *daemon*. If you will allow me, let me quote what he said about *The Soul's Code*: "In a nutshell, then, this book is about calling, about fate, about character, about innate image. Together they make up the 'acorn theory,' which holds that each person bears a uniqueness that asks to be lived and that is already present before it can be lived" (*The Soul's Code*, by James Hillman, p. 6). And although I agree with Hillman when he says *'your daemon is the carrier of your destiny,'* I have trouble squeezing his insight of the soul's code into the paradigm of one lifetime. That's too constricted and strains the credibility of his perspective. But when you see the soul's code in the context of many lifetimes—within the guiding principles of karma and reincarnation, that is—then the soul's code makes much more sense. Our *daemon* is the driving spirit of our soul's code, if you will; but I see much more in the spirit of our *daemon* than Hillman does. That's what I want to talk about."

"What you have caught a glimpse of in the spirit of the daemon was much too elusive for the Jungian analyst, but in the spirit of the creative process of active imagination, let's engage in this dialectic to bring a little more clarity to art and literature."

"Okay. Here's what I think our *daemon* is. I agree with Hillman that our *daemon* is the carrier of our destiny, but because I have embraced the principles of karma and reincarnation (which for me are not theory but a fact of life), our *daemon* becomes the carrier of both our encoded spiritual destiny and our karmic destiny; this is why our *daemon* can drive one mad in its effort to fulfill one's destined purpose, to which the biography of many artists can attest to given how driven they were by their *daemon*. I don't doubt this, Padre; because my *daemon* had such a powerful hold upon me that I was willing to pay any price to find my true self. But what does this have to do with literature, one may well ask?"

"Everything. But please explain further."

"As I've already pointed out with my own journey from the Body of God as an un-self-realized soul to my first primordial human lifetime where I gave birth to my reflective self-consciousness (at its most rudimentary) and on up to my current lifetime, I *know* that we are encoded with God's DNA to realize our divine nature, and this would be our soul's primary destiny; but because we have free will we create a karmic destiny that has to be fulfilled. This is what evolves into the spirit of our personal *daemon* that drives us to fulfill our destined purpose. In short, Padre; I think our personal *daemon* is the driving force of art and literature, because our *daemon* is the essential karmic truth of all the lives that we have lived and the meaning and purpose of our existential being. So when Macbeth tells us that life is a tale told by an idiot full of sound and fury signifying nothing, that is his **existential truth**; and when Wordsworth tells us that we come from God trailing clouds of glory, that is his **essential truth**. And when John Keats tells us that beauty is truth and truth beauty, that is his **existential/essential truth.** Our *daemon* is our personal truth that we realize from life to life, and when we have a surfeit of truth we are compelled to give it expression because that is our *daemonic* imperative, which is why writers *have* to write. 'I could feel a lump of painful truth pushing at my heart,' wrote Alice Munro in her story 'The Moons of Jupiter,' and this 'lump of painful truth' was her *daemonic* imperative. But I fear I haven't done this concept justice. Would you be kind enough to offer your perspective?"

"I would be happy to. An artist's daemon is all the meaning and purpose they have experienced in the course of their karmic history from one lifetime to the next, and when a writer has a surfeit of sacred meaning their daemon compels them to give it expression to satisfy their longing for wholeness and completeness. This is why writers describe their work as a journey of self-discovery. Writers seek the truth of life by engaging their imagination to magnify the truth of life, and in the process integrate the unconscious truth of their life with their conscious self and become more whole and complete. That's why your literary mentor loved writing more than any other activity of his life, and you know how much he loved big game hunting and deep sea fishing. Writing made Hemingway whole, but not enough to save him from himself. He was driven by his daemon, but his shadow had a much greater hold upon his life than his creative spirit. Does that help you?"

"A little, but not enough to satisfy my need to know. Maybe I should just abandon to my creative unconscious and let the chips fall where they may?"

"If you are willing to risk it, so am I."

"Don't make me laugh, Padre! You know where this book is going, just as you knew where my novel *Healing with Padre Pio* was going. You even told me that I was going to end my novel with a question, which to my complete surprise I did! (The question was *'Why bother?'*, which were the last words of *Healing with Padre Pio*.)

But I'm not going to press you on where this book is headed—as if you would tell me! Would you?"

"To the noblest virtue, my friend. That's all I can say."

"Fair enough. Now, on to the silent message of literature…"

17. THE SILENT MESSAGE OF LITERATURE

"The Way is the life force, which is Divine Spirit; and Divine Spirit speaks to each soul according to its needs..."

As hackneyed as the cliché may be, it's still true: we can lead a horse to water, but we can't make it drink. The horse has to do that on its own. In like manner, literature can lead us to the living water of life wisdom but it cannot make us drink. For example: "The Death of Ivan Ilych" has raised the awareness of many people from an unconscious feeling of relentless doubt and inauthenticity to a conscious awareness like Ivan Ilych (with all the consequent symptoms), but how many drank in the bitter/sweet truth of Ivan Ilych's experience?

As Jung said, it takes great moral courage to see our shadow—which Tolstoy did with his courageous story "The Death of Ivan Ilych" (I say courageous because I believe much of Tolstoy went into his character Ivan Ilych), but as provocative and enlightening as literature may be, it still cannot satisfy the longing in our soul for wholeness and completeness.

One can read the most inspiring poetry in the world—Wordsworth, Keats, Shelly, Whitman, Frost, Rumi, and Emily Dickinson to name a mere few; but not until one takes the silent message of poetry to heart will one satisfy their longing to be whole.

"He labors good on good to fix, and owes /To virtue every triumph that he knows," said William Wordsworth in his poem 'Character of the Happy Warrior,' but not until one puts to practice a life of virtue will one reap the benefits of the poem's message and satisfy the longing in their soul. Wordsworth brings us to the living water, but it's our choice to drink in the bitter/sweet wisdom of the poet's life experience.

I did, and the bitter/sweet truth of my own experience can be summed up in a saying that I wrought from living the life of a Happy Warrior: *"The shortest way to God is through hell!"* By this I mean the insufferable agony of authenticating myself by practicing a life of virtue—trying to be truthful, honest, kind, fair, and decent; because the harder I tried to live a life of virtue, the more my shadow resisted, which made my life pure hell.

In my efforts however, I awakened to the secret way of life inherent to human experience; that's how I became conscious of the silent message of literature, which in every writer's journey of self-discovery points to their essential nature. *"I, you, he, she, we, /In the garden of mystic lovers, /these are not true distinctions,"* said the mystic poet Rumi; the silent message being that our essential self and the *I Am* of God are one.

Rumi realized this, but he had help. He had the mysterious Shams of Tabriz to initiate him into the mystery of life's deepest secret. Rumi was a Sufi, and he practiced the Sufi art of "dying before dying." This is how he transformed the consciousness of his shadow and realized the *I Am* consciousness of his essential nature; and his poetry is replete with the bitter/sweet wisdom of his life experience.

But not the American writer Saul Bellow. "The aesthetic mystery of Bellow's achievement," said Professor Harold Bloom in *Novelists and Novels,* can be found in the heroes of his stories. "His heroes are superb observers, worthy of their Whitmanian heritage. What they lack is Whitman's Real Me or Me Myself, or else they are blocked from expressing it." But this too is the silent message of Bellow's bitter/sweet experience. Bellow failed to connect with his essential self and confirms the enormity of the effort it takes to become one's Real me or Me Myself; and as we learn from *Saul Bellow's Heart: A Son's Memoir,* by Bellow's son Greg, Saul died in moral conflict. "Was I a man or a jerk?" he asked his friend Gene Goodheart a day or so before dying; and he died unresolved in his shadow.

What, then, is the secret? What magical formula does the wisdom of literature point us to if not to a life of virtue which is the only way to make our two selves into one?

I've laid the groundwork, so I'm going to consult my Oracle to see if my creative unconscious has anything to add to this perspective; but before I consult my Oracle, I feel nudged to copy and paste my spiritual musing inspired by Saul Bellow's life: —

Was I a Man or a Jerk?
A Dying Writer's Last Question

I was online researching the Canadian-born American writer Saul Bellow, who won the Nobel Prize in Literature in 1976, and I came upon his son Greg Bellow talking about his memoir *Saul Bellow's Heart* that he wrote to show his father as he knew him growing up as opposed to the impression of the lionized writer that the public had of his famous father, and Greg related a fascinating anecdote about his father's dying question that peaked my interest enough to explore the moral implications of that question in today's spiritual musing.

Even to the very end, Saul Bellow was in moral conflict with himself; why else would he ask his friend for an honest answer to the question **"was I a man or a jerk?"** Although I have only read two of Saul Bellow's books, his novella *The Actual* and *It All Adds Up*, a nonfiction collection of some of his work which includes his Nobel Lecture, and one short story called "The Silver Plate," I never read any of his major novels like *Humbold's Gift, Herzog,* and *Mr. Sammler's Planet* (the one I want to read is *Ravelstein,* which was based on his friend and author of *The Closing of the American Mind,* Professor Alan Bloom), but after all of my research on Bellow and his novels and listening to Zachary Leader talk about his biography *The Life of Saul Bellow* I elicited a strong impression of the writer that gave me a context to the final question of his long-lived life**: "was I a man or a jerk?"**

Why would a man who spent his whole life exploring the human condition in his novels ask such a question if he did not have moral reservations about his life? But let me relate the anecdote first as his son Greg told it in the You Tube video JST Presents: "Saul Bellow's Spiritual Quest," and then I can explore his father's disturbing death-bed question.

A man in the audience asked Saul's son Greg Bellow the question, "I wonder if you know the manner of his dying? Were you with him when he died?"

DEATH, THE FINAL FRONTIER

"I was not," Greg replied; and then the man asked, "Did you hear about how he handled the occasion?" That's when Greg related the anecdote of his father's final question.

Saul Bellow was in his bed at home dying and tended to by his fifth wife Janice, who was forty years his junior, and he was in and out of consciousness and had not awakened in a couple of days when his friend Gene Goodheart came to visit him.

"Saul, Saul," said his friend, trying to wake him up, and Saul opened his eyes and saw his friend and said, "Gene, I want to ask you a question if you give me an honest answer."

"You know I'll give you an honest answer," said Gene Goodheart.

And Saul said, "Gene, was I a man or a jerk?"

We don't know what Gene Goodheart answered, but Saul's son Greg interpreted his father's question to mean that he was still wrestling with his conscience. "In other words, he had moral courage to the end, to be able to assess himself, to be able to criticize himself. That's what I know, and I don't think he lasted another few days," he replied to the man who asked Greg about his father's death; but if I were asked to give an answer to Saul Bellow's dying question, I would have to say: he was both.

Saul Bellow was the same as any other person in the world, only more exaggerated because he was a very gifted writer who explored his own conflicted nature through his novels; that's why he was awarded the Nobel Prize in Literature *"for the human understanding and subtle analysis of contemporary culture that are combined in his work."* Like every writer who taps into the consciousness of their times and becomes a witness to their generation, Saul Bellow reflected the human condition in his fiction as he experienced it in the inescapable dynamic of his Jewish heritage, mostly focused on Chicago where he lived, just as every writer explores the same human condition in the dynamic of their own heritage, like mine for example which is Italian Canadian; but why would I say that this Quebec-born American Jewish writer who sacrificed everyone for his art was both a man and a jerk? That's what I hope to explore in today's spiritual musing...

"One cannot tell writers what to do. The imagination must find its own path," wrote Saul Bellow in his Nobel Lecture; but the path that the writer takes may take him closer to the truth of the human condition than most people can bear. That's why Bellow added, "Perhaps humankind cannot bear too much reality, but neither can it bear too much unreality, too much abuse of the truth" (*It All Adds Up*, "The Nobel Lecture," p. 95); and that's the dilemma that every writer must suffer, because the closer they get to the truth of the human condition the harder it is to bear it, which was why Saul Bellow's conscience forced him on his deathbed to ask his friend Gene Goodheart **"was I a man or a jerk?"**

Just as an aside, if I may be allowed a moment of personal humor, I find the fact that Saul Bellow should ask a friend named Gene Goodheart for an honest answer to his deathbed question **"was I a man or a jerk?** to be so laden with irony that it would take a whole book to explain it; but it's enough to know that the spirit of synchronicity has a playful sense of humor, and why this unpredictable spirit has often been called the Trickster.

Being a writer, I am acutely conscious of the fact that we cannot escape what we are, which has been the inspiration for such great works of literature as *The Strange Case of Dr. Jekyll and Mr. Hyde* by Robert Louis Stevens, and *The Picture of Dorian Grey* by Oscar Wilde; and Saul Bellow could not escape the fact that he was as much of a jerk (perhaps more so, depending upon one's relationship with him) as he was the man he tried to be, or wanted the world to believe he was.

But that's the dilemma that art cannot resolve, which was why the gifted young writer Katherine Mansfield told her redoubtable editor A. R. Orage that "art is not enough" and why I wrote in my own memoir *The Pearl of Great Price*, **"Stories bear the truth of the human condition, and the human condition is the story of our becoming; but not until we solve the riddle of our becoming will literature resolve the issue of the human condition."**

Saul Bellow could not resolve the issue of his personal condition with the creative genius of his fiction, which is why he spent years studying the esoteric spiritual teachings of Rudolph Steiner, the founding father of Anthroposophy, and why Katherine Mansfield sought out the mystic teacher Gurdjieff at his Institute for the Harmonious Development of Man in Fontainebleau, France to study his radical teaching of self-transformation just before she died of tuberculosis.

But what is the central issue of the human condition that art cannot resolve? That's the question that writers feel with every fiber of their being but cannot resolve with their art but which they have to explore to give expression to that *lump of painful truth pushing at their heart*, as another Nobel laureate Alice Munro expressed the writer's compulsion to write; what is this lump of painful truth that has to find expression in a writer's work?

The prescient literary critic Professor Harold Bloom, author of *Novelists and Novels*, among many other brilliant books of literary criticism, caught a glimpse of this lump of painful truth pushing at Saul Bellow's heart and had this to say about the aesthetic mystery of Bellow's literary achievement: "His heroes are superb observers, worthy of their Whitmanian heritage. What they lack is Whitman's Real Me or Me Myself, or else they are blocked from expressing it" (*Novelists and Novels*, p. 419).

This "Real Me or Me Myself" is that lump of painful truth forever pushing at the writer's heart and what they seek with their fiction, which became the theme of my book *The Lion that Swallowed Hemingway*, because like Saul Bellow my literary mentor and high school hero Ernest Hemingway also died unresolved, which he confessed to in his memoir *A Moveable Feast*, the book that he was working on just before taking his own life with his favorite shotgun.

"When I saw my wife again standing by the tracks as the train came in by the piled logs at the station, I wish I had died before I ever loved anyone but her," wrote Hemingway at the end of *A Moveable Feast*, speaking of his first wife Hadley Richardson whom he betrayed with his affair with Pauline Pfeiffer, the woman who seduced and stole him away from Hadley but who was to be replaced by the journalist Martha Gellhorn, and she by his fourth wife Mary Welsh; and Saul Bellow's son Greg tells us in his memoir *Saul Bellow's Heart* that his father confessed to him that he wished he had never divorced Greg's mother, his first wife; but he did divorce her, and four more wives later he's in bed dying full of remorse and regrets.

And if I may, risking the esoteric flavor of my humor, I honestly feel that Saul Bellow's friend Gene Goodheart was providentially sent to visit Saul on his deathbed to let him know, in that synchronistic trickster way, that **lacking in the virtues of a good heart one will always risk being a jerk in life**. It was like the medieval morality play *The Summoning of Everyman* and **Mr. Good Heart** went to Saul, who was also summoned by God for a reckoning, and found him lacking in the virtues of a good heart, and the delicious irony of Saul Bellow's life was that he failed to see his answer to his dying question in his good friend Gene Goodheart's name!

———

"That was my spiritual musing. I hope you don't mind, Padre; but I'd like to engage you in a dialogue on the silent message of literature. Are you up to a little discourse?"

"It's not like I have nothing to do over here, but certainly; let's talk about the silent message of literature. But you have presented a strong case already, and I don't know what more I can add to help your reader understand the value of literature."

"I agree. There is only so much one can say about the bitter/sweet wisdom of life; but what the reader doesn't know is that the silent message of an author's bitter/sweet wisdom speaks the omniscient guiding principle of life; so if we can, let's try to tie this in with my theme on the final frontier of life."

"Jesus called the omniscient guiding principle of life the Way. The Way is what you call the secret way of life. I believe you got this term from Doctor Jung."

"Yes. From his commentary to *The Secret of the Golden Flower* that his friend Richard Wilhelm had sent him. This book was Jung's serendipitous confirmation of his studies of the Gnostic texts that concealed the mystic path to one's higher self that is central to the esoteric teachings of the Taoist philosophy found in *The Secret of the Golden Flower*. Jung was jubilant when he received this book from Richard Wilhelm, as would anyone be when serendipity comes knocking on their door; but let's get back to the point."

"And what would you say the point is?"

"That life has inherent purpose and meaning."

DEATH, THE FINAL FRONTIER

"Which is?"

"To realize the *I Am* consciousness of God."

"How?"

"Through the evolution of life. It was my experience— which I drew from my past-life regressions—that we come into this world as sparks of divine consciousness, or as embryonic souls if you will, to evolve through the life process for the purpose of individuating the *I Am* consciousness of God. In the simplest terms possible, I concluded that our purpose in life is to become what we are meant to be, a God-realized soul. This sounds airy-fairy mystical, but this is where the logic of my personal quest has taken me."

"And how would you tie this in with the theme of our book?"

"Our book? Okay, I can accept that. Well, as blunt as it may sound, death opens the door for soul to be born again into another body so it can continue its journey to wholeness and completeness. Death is the end of our existential life, but not the end of our essential life. Our essential life is the *I Am* consciousness of our individuating soul self, and our purpose is to grow in our own identity until we realize our divine nature. This is another reason why I respect Jung so much, because he placed the highest value on the individual self which he also believed to be the individuation of the Self of God."

"What more can I add?"

"That's it? You're not going to add to my insights with the bitter/sweet wisdom of your own agonizing experience of living with the stigmata for fifty years? You must be—and I know you are, because I experienced you while writing my novel *Healing with Padre Pio!* —brimming with all kinds of life wisdom. Just one drop, if you would?"

"For you my friend, a whole stream. But for now, let's just say that the Way is everywhere to be found in human experience. The Way is the life force, which is Divine Spirit; and Divine Spirit speaks to each soul according to its needs. This is why we all have different life experiences, and why our bitter/sweet wisdom is so individual—"

"Which is why we love to read literature! Every writer has their own bitter/sweet wisdom, and each writer's life wisdom is their individual way to the promised land. We all want to get to the promised land of our true self that Jesus called 'the pearl of great price,' and literature points the way with each author's personal journey to wholeness and completeness. Which is why some people can't get enough of literature—until they hit the brick wall of their own shadow, like Tolstoy did with 'The Death of Ivan Ilych.' Then life gets really interesting. And if I may, Padre; I'd like to quote a poem that I wrote that speaks to the bitter/sweet wisdom of literature."

"Poetry does cut to the quick. By all means, let us hear your poem."

"But you'll have to pardon the poet's presumption."

"It's not a presumption, my friend. It's the artist's imperative."

"Here's my poem, then: —

The Pearl of Great Price

Take the ore of your life and smelt it down,
and you have sacred meaning, the spiritual gold
of our destined purpose, —

Take the ore of your life and smelt it down,
and you have sacred knowledge, the magic elixir
of literature, —

Take the ore of your life and smelt it down,
and you have sacred suffering, the mystical marriage
of our lower and higher self, —

The Pearl of Great Price!

"Imperative or presumption, I don't know; but this is what the bitter/sweet ore of my life smelted down to."
"On that note, we can call it a day..."

18. THE FEAR OF DEATH

"We are all an I of God..."

As serendipity would have it, I picked up the *July/August 2016* issue of *Zoomer* magazine the other day that had a cover story titled "Fade to Black: Why it's Time to Rebrand Death" which dealt primarily with the issue of dying, how to prepare for it; but the comment that caught my attention was the following: "What keeps people from facing their mortality? Partly it's their anxiety about what, if anything, comes next." But if we are all sparks of God, divine and immortal in our essential nature, why are we so afraid of death and dying?

From my perspective, the answer is simple: we experience life from our existential self, which is mortal. And as our existential self faces death, it fears extinction; and the thought of being no more terrifies us. But because we have an immortal essential self we are anxious to know what (*if anything*, says our doubting existential self) comes after death.

This is man's dilemma, then: how do we reconcile the doubt and fear of our mortal existential self with our immortal essential self?

The American writer Don DeLillo's new novel *Zero K* deals with the question of our mortality, but from the perspective of our mortal existential self. The theme of this novel is about prolonging the mortal life of our existential self by scientific means. Two central characters seek to conquer death by submitting to it. They plan to be "chemically induced to expire" and frozen at a super secret cryonics compound so that one day they might be resurrected through a yet-to-be perfected science involving cellular regeneration and nanotechnology. DeLillo pushes the envelope even further: one day humans (at least the very rich) will have the option of being reborn as new and improved beings implanted with memories of their choice—music, philosophical writings, family photographs, "Russian novels, the films of Bergman, Kubrick, Kurosawa, Tarkovsky."

That's the target plot of *Zero K*, a futuristic look at extending our mortal existential life through science, which may very well happen one day in the distant future; but what about our essential self, our immortal divine essence? What happens to our soul? Where did it go in *Zero K*? Where is it right now? Are we so confined by the consciousness of our mortal existential self that we are blind to our immortal essential self?

This brings me back to where I started this book, to Jeanne Van Bronkhorst's *Dreams at the Threshold*. "Dreams are the guiding words of the soul," said the eminent psychologist Carl Jung, and Jeanne Van Bronkhorst's book illustrates the comforting guidance that dreams have given many of her dying clients.

Listening to our dreams is the message of *Dreams at the Threshold*, because they give us the comforting guidance we need to allay the fears of our mortal existential self. Dreams confirm the reality of our essential nature, which Jung realized in his lifelong study of the dreaming process (he analyzed over eighty thousand dreams in his long career as a psychotherapist), and this confirmed for him the superstition of all times and races that the dream has been regarded as a truth-telling oracle, because whenever he didn't know how to proceed with a client he always listened to his client's dreams for guidance.

That's exactly what social worker Jeanne Van Bronkhorst learned to do, which became the inspiration for her book *Dreams at the Threshold*. One day she was visiting another client who had politely answered "fine, fine" to her questions about her emotional coping, but instead of moving on to the purpose of her visit Jeanne decided to ask her client, "How are your dreams these days?" Little did she expect that this simple question would open up a door to the comforting guiding words of the soul: —

"That simple question launched me into a new relationship with clients and their dreams. Asking about dreams opened us easily into conversations about their most pressing concerns as well as the larger questions of life—conversations I had not found by asking about pain or eating habits…You may wonder, if dreams are such an amazing help at the end of life, why aren't more people working with dreams? Why has no one noticed this earlier? The answer has more to do with modern Western culture than with our dreams" (*Dreams at the Threshold*, Jeanne Van Bronkhorst, pp. 4-5).

If I may digress for a moment (actually, it's not a digression; it's more of a confirmation of *the omniscient guiding principle of life*), why was Jeanne Van Bronkhorst inspired to ask that simple question which opened up a whole new dimension of comfort and healing with her clients if not because the guiding principle of her life wanted her to explore the mystery of death and dying and expand the parameters of her palliative care healing skills?

As I've already said—a conclusion that was forced upon me by my own bitter/sweet experiences in my quest for an answer to the meaning and purpose of life—when we're ready to move on to another path on our journey to wholeness and completeness *the omniscient guiding principle of life* provides us with an opportunity, as it did with Jeanne Van Bronkhorst when for no apparent reason she asked one of her clients that question "How are your dreams these days?" This simple question changed her life.

But this is how serendipity works. Just ask Doctor L. Brian Weiss, author of the international best-seller *Many Lives, Many Masters*; because a serendipitous experience with one of his clients opened up his healing practice so wide that he's now a world authority on healing through the practice of past-life regression therapy. And I could cite many more examples of how merciful serendipity changed the lives of many people, which I have done in my four volumes of spiritual musings, primarily my final volume *The Armchair Guru*; so I need not expound upon the presence in our lives of *the omniscient guiding principle of life*, because it's always there to guide us when we need it.

But as Jeanne Van Bronkhorst implied, our modern Western culture stifles the voice of soul when it speaks to us. "Oh, it's just a dream," one says, cavalierly dismissing the guidance of their soul which knows what's best for our journey of self-discovery. This is the irony of the modern world; we are so preoccupied with extending our mortal existential life that we have stopped paying attention to our immortal essential self. Why else would churches be losing attendance? A young Pilipino woman down the street married to a Caucasian who brought her nine-month old son to church one Sunday said to me later in the day, "I never see young people at church. Only old people. And not very many old people."

Whether this has something to say about the Christian religion, which I think it does, it speaks to the modern world's preoccupation with something else; and what this something else is, no-one seems to know. But our dreams know. Our dreams speak *the omniscient guiding principle of life*, and if we listen to our dreams we will get the guidance we need to negotiate our journey to wholeness and completeness. But just for good measure, let me run this by my Oracle to see what St. Padre Pio has to say…

"As always, I didn't expect to be opening up the subject of dreams in this chapter; but as you know, I trust my creative unconscious to guide my writing. So if I may, let's kick this up a notch and be a little more conscious of where this book is going. After all, isn't the whole purpose of this exercise to make myself (and the reader) more conscious—as it did Carl Jung, for example? He said that his confrontation with the unconscious (which he later came to call an exercise in active imagination) gave him the major ideas of his psychology, which he still had not exhausted before he died; so cannot I expect the same with our discussions?"

"Haven't you already?"

"Yes, of course. All I'm trying to say is that by engaging my Oracle (personified as you, St. Padre Pio), I'm engaging my creative unconscious—right?"

"Yes."

"And this automatically raises my level of awareness?"

"It does. This is the purpose of this exercise. So what's your point?"

"Are you asking because you want to assert the distinction between who I am and who you are? Are you not my creative unconscious?"

"We've discussed this already. But for good measure, we are all an I of God, and being an I of God we are all one; ergo, I have my own distinct personality as Padre Pio (which presupposes my own history of the many lives I lived in the world), but being an I of God like yourself, and everyone else for that matter, then you would be correct in saying that your creative unconscious and I are one. This is

DEATH, THE FINAL FRONTIER

why Dr. Jung eventually came to call the spiritual guide Philemon that he met in his active imagination experience his Higher Self. Philemon was Carl Jung's essential self, but it took him a long time to see it; just as it's taking you a long time to see that we are also one."

"But distinct?"

"Yes. This is the mystery of the I of God. This is what Rumi meant with the verse you quoted. 'I, you, he, she, we, /In the garden of mystic lovers, /these are not true distinctions.' Now why don't you look up the verse where Rumi makes the distinction between man's existential self and his essential self. I'll wait..."

"That's in the same book. *The Language of Life,* by Bill Moyers. Okay, let me check it out...Here it is. Let me quote it: *"These leaves, our bodily personalities, seem identical, /but the globe of soul-fruit /we make, /each is elaborately unique."* And you know what, Padre; this brings our chapter on the fear of death to closure very nicely, because the genius of Rumi's poetry confirms the distinction between our mortal existential self and our immortal essential self, and depending upon how centered one is in their existential self determines the degree of their fear of death and dying. And the question now is: how can we reconcile our existential self with our essential self so we can allay our fear of death and dying?"

"Let that be your next chapter."

"And so it shall...

19. THE GREAT RECONCILIATION

"Today's reality is all about facing the final hour..."

Let's get it out of the way as quickly as possible: there can never be a reconciliation of our mortal existential self with our immortal essential self through scientific means—not even with the scientific manipulation of vibrations, because this great reconciliation has to be voluntary, BORN OF OUR OWN FREE WILL!

I have no doubt that Penny Peirce is on the money with her intuitive understanding of the power of personal vibrations, which she discusses in her book *Frequency* (and more fully in her follow-up book *Leap of Perception, The Transforming Power of Your Attention*), but "the habit of soul gathering and collecting herself into herself," as Socrates calls the great reconciliation of our existential self with our essential self, has to be done through an act of personal will, a choice made to transform (Socrates calls it "purification" in the *Phaedo*) the consciousness of our existential self which can only be done by living a life of virtue—which Socrates also confirms, believing Goodness to be the most noble of the virtues.

I also believe Goodness to be the most noble virtue; which is why I summed up my long and insufferable journey to my true self in the simple realization that the fundamental purpose of life is to be a good person, because **_being a good person initiates the process of self-purification which reconciles our existential self with our essential self._** So it doesn't matter how scientifically evolved we become, we can't short-circuit the great reconciliation process of our evolution. This is why teachers of the sacred knowledge maintain that man must complete what nature cannot finish; which is what attracted me to Gurdjieff's teaching that I wrote about in *Gurdjieff Was Wrong but His Teaching Works*.

In *Living Beyond the Five Senses, The Emergence of a Spiritual Being*, psychologist Teresa Decicco writes: "The journey to *Homo nuovo* is one with many roads but they all eventually lead to the same place." And where is this same place if not to conscious evolution, which means taking the initiative to purify the consciousness of our mortal existential self. That's why Teresa Decicco called her book *Living Beyond the Five Senses*, because she realizes that *Homo nuovo*, our emerging spiritual being, demands a way of life that "collects and gathers" itself unto itself, a way of life that the pioneer researcher on death and dying Doctor Elisabeth Kubler-Ross beautifully expressed in the simple words of "love and service." In her autobiography *The Wheel of Life, A Memoir of Living and Dying*, she too saw that "all destiny leads down the same path—growth, love and service," confirming the sacred knowledge that life will only evolve us so far, and no further. To complete what nature cannot finish, we have to take evolution into our own hands and initiate the process that my creative unconscious has so aptly called the great reconciliation...

Even though whole schools of thought have evolved to explain the dynamics of the great reconciliation, like the mystical path of Sufism and Gurdjieff's system, I wrote a short poem to capture the gist of this mystical marriage of our two selves: —

Alchemy of the Self

The agony of my life was being
a stranger to myself, because the
person who was me was not the
person I wanted to be; so I broke
the mirror of my life and suffered
the pain of putting myself together
again into the person I was meant
to be; and now I no longer suffer
the agony of being a stranger to
myself, because I *am* me

Without going into detail, which I've done in *The Summoning of Noman*, I had an impulsive sexual experience that shocked my conscience and woke me up to my false self; and I dedicated the rest of my life to finding my true self or die trying. One path led to another, until serendipity brought Gurdjieff into my life; and with his teaching of "work on oneself" I reconstituted myself into the person I was meant to be.

The premise of Gurdjieff's teaching is that man is not born with an immortal soul, but with the right kind of effort one can "create" his own soul. In effect, for Gurdjieff man is a mortal existential being without an essential immortal self; but with *conscious effort* and *intentional suffering* (and other techniques like *self-remembering* and *non-identifying*), one can transform their consciousness and realize an immortal soul.

I lived Gurdjieff's teaching with single-minded conviction (in retrospect, I would call my commitment pathological because I was hell-bent on finding my true self), and I did transform the consciousness of my mortal being enough to realize my immortal nature, which I experienced one day in my mother's kitchen while she was kneading bread dough on the kitchen table; so I know that Gurdjieff's teaching works.

Even though I doubted the premise of his teaching, it was the right teaching for me to find my true self; and after I had my regression to the Body of God where all souls come from, I ended up writing *Gurdjieff Was Wrong but His Teaching Works* because I wanted to credit Gurdjieff for his teaching despite his misperception that man is not born with an immortal soul. We are all immortal sparks of God, but we aren't aware of it; and becoming aware of our essential self is what the great reconciliation is all about.

This is what the sayings and parables of Jesus are about, despite how watered down his teaching has become; but as Jesus said, one has to live his sayings for them to work their magic of transforming the consciousness of our mortal existential self.

"Therefore whosoever heareth these sayings of mine, and doeth them, I will liken him unto a wise man, which built his house upon a rock," said Jesus, with the genius of metaphor that reveals the alchemy of his sayings when put into practice; and as esoteric and mystical as Christ's sayings and parables may sound, all they do when put into practice is reconcile our existential self with our essential self, as any ethical system will do when it is lived with passionate sincerity. And when one transforms his consciousness enough to shift his center of gravity from his mortal existential self to his immortal essential self, he will experience the great reconciliation and realize his immortal nature.

This is what the sacred knowledge calls the "mystical marriage," which is central to the ancient Taoist text *The Secret of the Golden Flower* that confirmed Carl Jung's studies of the sacred knowledge. "I was completely ignorant of Chinese philosophy, and only later did my professional experience show me that in my technique I had been unconsciously led along that secret way which has been the preoccupation of the best minds of the East for centuries," wrote Jung in his commentary to *The Secret of the Golden Flower*, and by "secret way" he meant what I came to recognize as *the omniscient guiding principle of life*.

Jesus called the great reconciliation "making the two into one," meaning our lower existential self and higher essential self; but this requires *conscious effort*, which only those that have a desperate longing in their soul for wholeness and completeness will make. Do you have any thoughts on this, Padre?

"One or two. What you call the great reconciliation, I called my glory when I was a lowly friar in the monastery in San Giovani Rotondo."

"I know. I read that in several biographies of your life. You couldn't suffer enough for Jesus, and in your suffering you experienced the great reconciliation—or, as you put it, your glory; but let's see if we can explain this mystical process in the simplest terms possible. Would you like to give it try?"

"Let's call suffering the purifying fire of the soul. And what does suffering purify?"

"You're asking me?"

"Yes."

"The spiritually impure consciousness of our mortal existential self."

"And what makes it spiritually impure?"

"Given the logic of my dialectic, I'd have to say it's the consciousness of our mortal nature. By some mystical process of spiritual alchemy, suffering immortalizes the consciousness of our existential mortal nature, which is why I think you called it your glory."

"Thank you for explaining that. Yes, suffering was my glory. And I couldn't get enough glory in my lifetime. You may find this hard to believe, but I died in want of glory."

"Come on, Padre! Are you suggesting that there's no end to the great reconciliation?"

"Not at all. I simply couldn't get enough of God's love."

"Are you saying that suffering is God's love in action?"

"That's exactly what I'm saying."

"Is this why Jesus said to Philemon in Jung's *Red Book* that he had brought the beauty of suffering to the world? Is the beauty of suffering God's love for man?"

"Yes."

"This is too deep, Padre. No one will believe it."

"Possibly. But given the context of our dialectic, it makes sense."

"That's what Carl Jung said about dreams. Only in the context of one's life can dreams be understood. So if suffering does immortalize the consciousness of our mortal human self, then it would make perfect sense to see it as God's love in action. Still, Padre; given society's antipathy today for anything spiritual, this would be a hard sell."

"When faced with the final hour, one's heart opens to the mysteries. Don't sell your readers short. Today's reality is all about facing the final hour. Turn on your TV and what do you have? Death is everywhere. This is the consciousness of the times. What the world needs is a spiritual context for man's life, which we're providing. Any more questions?

"No, I don't think so."

"Then we can call it a day. And don't worry about your next chapter. It will come to you in the course of your daily functions..."

20. LET'S TALK TURKEY

"The fear of death intensifies one's life experience..."

For over five decades I've been reading books that I was led to read by my intuitive guiding principle to satisfy the longing in my soul for the meaning and purpose of life—*not only did I want to know who I was, but why I was and where I came from*—and after these many years I have satisfied my inner longing; but sad to say, the answers that I found cannot be proven because there is only self-initiation into the mysteries of life.

This is tragic, because when one finds an answer to life's imponderable questions one has an almost messianic need to share his truth; but the more one tries to share his truth, the more resistance one gets from the world. But why?

I pondered this problem for years. And then I read *Selected Letters of C. G. Jung, 1909-1961*, and I found my answer in a letter that he wrote to Hans Schmid (*November 6, 1915*) in which he revealed how he found the answer to my peculiar problem—a problem that vexed him more than me and which he deftly defined as man's "resistance to understanding."

St. Brigitta of Sweden (*1303-1373*) helped Jung gain the insight to man's resistance to understanding with a vision she had of the devil who spoke to God about the psychology of devils. Their greed was boundless but could not be sated, and Jung intuited that understanding was a devourer like the devil which could not be satisfied and that man has a natural resistance to being devoured by understanding.

"Understanding is a fearfully binding power, at times a veritable murder of the soul as soon as it flattens out vitally important differences. The core of the individual is a mystery of life, which is snuffed out when it is 'grasped,'" wrote Jung to Hans Schmid; and finally it made sense to me why man has a natural resistance to understanding.

This is deep, and I don't know if I can explain what Jung meant by man's resistance to understanding; but I do know something about the shadow. And it is the shadow side of man's personality that does not want to be devoured by understanding, because understanding threatens the shadow's existence. This is the root source of man's unbelief.

The shadow is the unconscious side of our ego personality, and over time the shadow develops its own identity separate from our ego personality; but the shadow self is not real, as such. It's real psychically, but because it is made up of the unconscious energy of our ego personality its very existence is threatened when it is made conscious. This is why man has a resistance to understanding anything that poses a threat to his shadow identity, like the materialist who keeps denying the reality of life after death despite all the evidence that has been gathered by reputable people like Dr. Elisabeth Kubler Ross, Dr. Raymond Moody, Dr. Ian Stevenson, Dr. Michael Newton, Dr. Brian L. Weiss, and social workers like Jeanne Van Bronkhorst to name a mere few.

People *are* what they believe, but what if one's beliefs are false? One can deny the existence of the immortal soul and the afterlife all they want, but what if they are facing their final hour and have what Jeanne Van Bronkhorst calls "Preparation Dreams" to help them get ready for their imminent death? She writes in *Dreams at the Threshold*: "At their deepest level, dreams at the end of life underline an assumption that we are more than our physical bodies and that who we are transcends if not our physical death, then certainly our dying. Our dreams view dying as the next great emotional and spiritual challenge to face and accept."

And what if one has "Visitation Dreams" where one's deceased relatives come to visit them before dying? Jeanne has many stories of people who had these dreams, and some visitations weren't even dreams at all; many were wide awake when one's dear ones came to visit them to comfort them on their journey to the other side. Does one dismiss these visitation experiences as fantasies induced by medication?

Staunch unbelievers would dismiss them because they don't want their unbelief (shadow) to be swallowed up and snuffed out, but not the person who has these experiences; they are so real to them that they cannot dismiss them as fantasies or hallucinations. These visitations from loved ones are a part of their reality, just like any other experience in their life; this is what Gurdjieff meant by self-initiation into the mysteries of life.

But this begs the question about our beliefs. What are they made of if they are false? For that matter, what is our shadow self made of? Given the amount of energy that's being poured into the study of the shadow (one of the best books being *Meeting the Shadow, The Hidden Power of the Dark Side of Human Nature*, edited by Connie Zweig and Jeremiah Abrams), psychology no longer questions the shadow's existence; but what is it made of?

This goes to the physics (or metaphysics) of consciousness, and that's too far advanced for me to answer; but I have answered this mind-boggling question from a philosophical perspective, and I can confidently say that the shadow side of our ego personality is made of the *non-being* consciousness of our ontological nature, which is what makes it such a paradoxical creature because our shadow self is real in its *non-being*.

As idiotic as it may appear to be, our shadow self is who we are not and not who we are. Or as Jung simply put it, our shadow is what we don't want to be, which is why we repress our shadow to the depths of our unconscious and try to forget about it.

But to satisfy the longing in our soul (teleological imperative, actually) for wholeness and completeness, we have to integrate our unconscious shadow into our conscious ego personality, which the shadow refuses to do; this is why man is always in conflict with himself, as Tolstoy illustrated with his story "The Death of Ivan Ilych."

So if our shadow is made up of the consciousness of our *non-being*, then it is by its very nature non-real and inauthentic and can justly be called our false personality. But because our false personality is so tightly interwoven with our ego personality we cannot tell which is which. This is why Jung said that it takes great moral courage to see our shadow, and even more courage to resolve it by consciously integrating it into our ego personality.

Inspired by John Freeman's iconic BBC *Face to Face* interview with Carl Jung, I wrote a poem to address man's natural resistance to understanding:

Interview with a Shaman

"Only ignorance
denies these things,"
said the shaman to the head
on the pole;
I don't need to believe,
I know."

The path was difficult,
far away and deep, and
his guide a winged fantasy;
but archival wisdom and
serendipity saved the day,
and sanity prevailed.

"But surely, death is an end?"
the head on the pole refrained;
but with a twinkle in his eye,
the shaman replied: "Yes,
it is an end. "And there we
are not quite certain."

And so it went…

There are far too many stories that part the veil of life and give us a glimpse into the afterlife (as Jeanne Van Bronkhorst has provided with *Dreams at the Threshold*) to not take them seriously; and there are far too many stories of NDEs (near-death experiences) for people to doubt in the existence of an immortal soul (*Proof of Heaven, A Neurosurgeon's Journey into the Afterlife*, by Eben Alexander, M. D., which according to Dr. Raymond Moody is "living proof of an afterlife"); and there are far too many stories of reincarnation (many of which were proven by Dr. Ian Stevenson) to doubt that we have lived before; and there are far too many stories of people experiencing extraordinary coincidence that have changed their lives (*The Synchronicity Key* by David Wilcock being one of the most comprehensive books on the subject) to not seriously consider that we are all guided by an intelligent principle that comes to our assistance whenever we're in desperate need of guidance, as I have been many times in my life; and yet man continues to flounder in doubt. This is why I've adopted *"Life is an individual journey"* as my personal motto…

"Your thoughts, Padre?"

"You've covered a lot of ground in this chapter, but I do have one thought I'd like to share with your reader. The fear of death intensifies one's life experience, and in that sense it's very effective for getting the most out of life. But the downside is that fear of death can also paralyze one's spirit, and this can take the joy out of living."

"So it's a question of finding the right balance?"

"If at all possible, yes."

"Pardon me, Padre; but I have to ask you something now that I don't know how to address but which has to be addressed to round off the picture of man's fear of death. We've laid the foundation, so here goes: can a person be born false?"

"Why do you ask?"

"Because I was born false. Well, not particularly; but my shadow came out in my teens and possessed my personality. That's what my book *The Summoning of Noman* explored."

"Yes, and much more. Your question is very probing, but it is necessary to complete the picture that we are drawing of soul's individuation. To answer your question, no one is born false because one's false personality is unconscious and does not come out until the circumstances of one's new incarnation brings it out. That's what happened to you. You were born into a family dynamic that made it highly likely that your false personality would break loose from your unconscious, which it did with your traumatic sexual experience. But that's what you needed to begin your quest for your true self. So you're quite right in your motto, because every soul's journey to wholeness is individual and leads to the great reconciliation eventually; but because the individuating consciousness of man's existential self is both being and non-being, man is always in a state of becoming. He both is and is not what he is, which can be very confusing to the individual. This is the problem that existential

philosophers like Soren Kierkegaard and Jean Paul Sartre tried to resolve but couldn't. The only resolution to man's existential problem is the sacred knowledge of the self. This is why you were called to write this book on the final frontier of life. But don't force your subject on your reader. Let the spirit of your book guide you."

"Fair enough. Just one more question, if I may?"

"Certainly."

"Who cares? Why should I even bother with this book?"

"Where would you be if not for books? Books open pathways for the soul, and this book was meant to be written. Don't ever question your inspiration. That would be blasphemy."

"Blasphemy? That's a bit harsh."

"A calling is a calling, and turning one's back on one's calling blasphemes Holy Spirit. This is why Jesus cursed the fig tree. The fig tree was not true to its calling. But we can talk about this later. Do you have any more concerns?"

"I've been chastened enough, thank you. I'll get back to you when I'm called."

"You do amuse me, my friend. Have a wonderful day…"

21. THE FIG TREE THAT JESUS CURSED

"Man's greatest need in life is to be what he is meant to be..."

Why did Jesus curse the fig tree? No one knows for sure, but I have my suspicion that Jesus was pointing to the essential purpose of his mission to help man complete what nature cannot finish and liberate soul from its prison...

Victor E. Frankl wrote *Man's Search for Meaning*, a portrait of man's soul stripped bare in the horrific concentration camps of Nazi Germany, a remarkable book which posits that man's fundamental need in life is to know the reason for his being, and which the young psychiatrist Dr. Frankl reduced to man's search for meaning (and from which was born his insightful healing modality of Logotherapy); but given my experience of the individuation process, I have to take Dr. Frankl's insight a step further and posit that man's fundamental need in life is to become what he is meant to be—his essential self.

No one can deny that man is driven by a need to know the meaning of life—why suffering, evil, love, greed and a million and one things, an inherent need that was intensely magnified in the concentration camps by the evil perpetrated by the Nazis upon the Jewish prisoners; but man's will for meaning is born of man's *a priori* need to become what we are meant to be—the teleological impulse of our essential nature that is the reason for our being.

We are born with an impulse to become what we are meant to be, just as an acorn seed has an impulse to become an oak tree; and we become what we are meant to be through living. It doesn't matter what we do—eating, drinking, having sex, working, arguing, praying, whatever—the mere act of living nourishes the individuation process of our essential self and fulfills our destined purpose of becoming what we are meant to be.

But, sadly, the mere act of living cannot satisfy the longing in our soul for wholeness and completeness, regardless how much living we do. We can intensify the life we live, as many people do when they become addicted to life like runners who have to have their daily running fix (I speak from experience of running seven miles a day for years), or the businessman who cannot make enough money and must grow his business, but it doesn't matter how much lust we have for life, it will never satisfy the longing in our soul to become what we are meant to be. But why? Why cannot life satisfy our longing to be whole?

This is our dilemma, which I will address after I copy and paste my spiritual musing that was inspired by Victor Frankl's book *Man's Search for Meaning*, because Frankl's book draws such a strong distinction between our existential self and our essential self that it cries out for resolution, which seems to be the dialectical purpose of this book: —

Man's Will to Be

"Man does not simply exist but always decides what his existence will be, what he will become in the next moment."

Man's Search for Meaning
Victor Frankl

Not all of my spiritual musings come to me in a synoptic vision wherein I see the whole truth of my idea and then have to work it out in the writing (and not without considerable thought and effort, I might add); some, if not most of my spiritual musing insights have to gestate in my unconscious for months and often years before they take seed and sprout in the soil of my conscious mind to grow and blossom into their full meaning, like the insight for today's spiritual musing on *man's will to be*.

This dynamic between my creative unconscious and conscious mind goes to the very heart of writing my spiritual musings, which I have to reflect upon for a moment or two before I proceed with the idea of today's spiritual musing; not to detract from my musing, but to help explain the mystery of the creative process that is central to today's spiritual musing on *man's will to be*.

In my long and painful journey of self-discovery, I came to the simple realization that **man's greatest need in life is to be what he is meant to be**. This is an *a priori* need that exists before we even come into this world, and it drives all of our other needs like our need for air, water, food, sex, and emotional succor. This need to be what we are meant to be presupposes itself because it is encoded in our soul, just like the oak tree is presupposed in the acorn seed; and our purpose in life is to grow and become what we are meant to be. This is why Carl Jung said, *"As each plant grows from a seed and becomes in the end an oak tree, so man must become what he is meant to be. He ought to get there, but most get stuck."*

The biggest, and probably most important discovery of my entire life was the realization that we do not come into this world ready-made; we have to grow into what we are meant to be, which makes *becoming* what we are meant to be the very purpose of our existence, and what we are meant to be is our essential, spiritual self.

I've already explained in my spiritual musings (and in my book *The Pearl of Great Price*) why we come into this world with an *a priori* need to be our true self, which Jesus called "the pearl of great price," but the realization that came to me in my journey of self-discovery was that to be our true self we have to *become* our true self just as the oyster has to create its pearl from a tiny mineral fragment. That is what I meant by saying that we do not come into this world ready-made; we have to "create" our true self like the oyster creates its precious pearl. Our precious pearl is our true self, the evolving identity of our essential spiritual nature.

And this is where I part company with Christianity (but not Christ's teaching that addresses the dynamic of *becoming* our true self) which contends that our immortal soul is created at the moment of human conception and is ready-made, and Buddhism also which disavows the existence of an individual autonomous self altogether, and all non-duality teachings that categorically believe that we are one Self complete unto ourselves without having to go through the pilgrimage and penance stage of *becoming* our true self as Jesus taught with his sayings and parables; and we cannot *become* our true self without participating in the creative process of our *becoming*, which brings me back to the theme of *man's will to be*.

In effect, we have to work with our creative unconscious to *become* our true self, because this is how we grow in our spiritual nature; and even though this is a natural process that we go through despite ourselves (we are forever making decisions that involve the creative process of our unconscious mind), our inherent need to be cannot be satisfied without a strong *will to do*, because only through doing can we satisfy *our will to be*. This is why some people get "hooked" on life, like running, cycling, hiking, mountain climbing, gardening, and one's work even, because they have a voracious hunger to satisfy their *will to be* because the logic of life is that the more we do the more we *become* what we are meant to be.

This is how we *become* our true self through the natural process of evolution through karma and reincarnation; but—*and this is a very big but!*—we cannot satisfy the longing in our soul to be our true self through karma and reincarnation alone until we take evolution into our own hands, which we can only do with what Gurdjieff called *conscious effort* and *intentional suffering*—the Sufis call it "conscious dying," or "dying before dying," and Jesus expressed the same process of *becoming* our true self in his saying **"He that loveth his life shall lose it; and he that hateth his life in this world shall keep it unto life eternal."**

"Man must complete what nature cannot finish," said the ancient alchemists, the Gnostics of the soul; and it was this realization that man's greatest need in life is his *will to be* that added a deeper layer of meaning to the existential premise of

DEATH, THE FINAL FRONTIER

Frankl's book *Man's Search for Meaning* which posits that man's fundamental need in life is to know the reason for his being, which Dr. Frankl reduced to *"man's will to meaning."*

As I said, not all of my spiritual musings come to me synoptically, they gestate in my unconscious until they are ready to take seed in my conscious mind; and when they sprout in my conscious mind my Muse will find a way to assist the seed to grow and blossom into its full meaning, as it did when quite by "chance" I came across Victor Frankl's book *Man's Search for Meaning* while looking for Joseph Campbell's *The Hero with a Thousand Faces* in my basement library this summer and which I was strongly nudged to read; and as I read *Man's Search for Meaning* the seed of today's spiritual musing sprouted as *"man's will to be"* because it completed Dr. Frankl's *"will to meaning."* And this, if I may be allowed to say so, is how the collective unconscious works through the consciousness of the individual self to help expand and raise the consciousness of humanity.

Victor Frankl was a young psychiatrist when he was sent to the concentration camps by the Nazis in WW II, and like all the prisoners in the camps he suffered many humiliating indignities in the hands of his tormentors who stripped him to his primal, naked self; but out of his unthinkable physical and mental anguish was born his existential psychology of Logotherapy ("a meaning-centered psychotherapy") which has become a remarkable healing modality for tortured and conflicted souls that suffer unbearable loss of meaning.

The seemingly senseless nature of the brutal suffering that Victor Frankl and his fellow prisoners suffered in the hands of their evil captors in the concentration camps forced him to part the veil of life and see that the prisoners who had something to live for, even if only in their own mind, found meaning in their unbearable existence; but what gave them their *will to meaning* was the inherent teleological purpose of their life that they were born with, which is *man's will to be.*

In conclusion, we have a *will to meaning* because we have a *will to be* our true self, and no amount of suffering can extinguish the holy flame of our existence.

How then do we resolve the dilemma of our *will to meaning* (our existential self) and *our will to be* (our essential self)?

Doctor Frankl resolves the issues of our existential self with man's will *to meaning*, but he does not address the issue of *man's will to be all that he is meant to be*, which has turned out to be the very premise of this book.

In the book *Why I Write: Thoughts on the Craft of Fiction*, twenty-six personal essays by successful contemporary writers, the writer who best expresses the connective tissue of the creative process found in all these essays, which I've come to see as the transcendent function of the imagination, was Pat Conroy, author of *The Great Santini*.

In his essay "Stories," Pat Conroy comes the closest of any writer that I have read who "sees" (in the creative sense) that writing stories is his path to wholeness and completeness: "A novel is my fingerprint, my identity card, and the writing of a novel is one of the few ways I have found to approach the altar of God and creation itself. You try to worship God by performing the singularly courageous and impossible favor of knowing yourself," says Conroy, because writing is Conroy's path to wholeness, as it is for all writers; but writing will never satisfy the longing in one's soul to become what they are meant to be because writing cannot reconcile the existential self with the essential self and make the two into one.

"Literature is not enough," said the short story writer Katherine Mansfield, and by literature she meant writing literature as well as reading it—regardless of how much time, sweat and tears one pours into their writing. It's just not enough to satisfy the longing in one's soul to become what they are meant to be. *It's just not enough!*

Tolstoy tells us that he wrote his novels in his own blood, but it wasn't until he wrote "The Death of Ivan Ilych" that he saw what he had to do for the great reconciliation which would save him from himself, and his great epiphany while writing "The Death of Ivan

Ilych" caused significant spiritual upheaval in his life, as it would any person who confronts their false self as Tolstoy did through Ivan Ilych. This is the mystery, then: resolving the consciousness of our dual nature, and the inspiration for my poem: —

Stairway of Heaven

Poetry is the way to the great
reconciliation, slashing through
the forests of our brambled self.

Every word, image, and experience
shines a light into the darkness
of tomorrow, leaving a trail
for us to follow.

No one poet knows the way to the
end of our becoming, yet every
poem the poet writes adds a
new rung to the stairway
of heaven, the great
reconciliation!

    Can it be so simple, then? Did Jesus curse the fig tree simply because it was barren, because it wasn't what it was meant to be, a fruit-bearing tree, and Jesus was speaking in parable about the purpose of man's existence? And what is the purpose of man's existence if not to bear the fruit of his own divine nature, which Jesus called being born again in spirit? Was Jesus pointing to the barren life of the existential self by cursing the fig tree?

    But what if it wasn't the season for the fig tree to bear fruit? We don't know that, do we? Every tree bears fruit in its own season, but what is the season for man to bear the fruit of his own being? Did Jesus curse the fig tree to draw attention to man's nature? Was he telling his disciples that the life of man is barren until it bears the fruit of its divine nature, which man must do by having faith? ***"Truly I tell you, if you have faith and do not doubt, not only can you do what was done to the fig tree, but also you can say to this mountain, 'Go,*** *throw yourself into the sea,' and it will be done. If you believe, you will receive whatever you ask for in prayer,"* said Jesus to his disciples (Matthew 21: 21-22).

Reconciling our existential self with our essential self *is* the core teaching of Christ's sayings and parables, which he referred to as making the two into one; but man must believe that this is possible. Did Jesus curse the fig tree as an object lesson for his disciples to see that with faith man can do miracles? And what greater miracle for man than to bear the fruit of his divine nature? I honestly don't know, but I can consult my Oracle...

"What do you have to say about this, Padre?"

"You are much closer to the truth than you realize. Yes, Jesus did curse the fig tree; and if the tree was in fruit-bearing season or not, it does not matter for what Jesus intended. Jesus wanted to teach his disciples about the power of faith. His mission was to bring a teaching of faith into the world, which he taught by example. It's hard for people to believe that Jesus did all of those miracles, but he did do them. And he cursed the fig tree to let his disciples know that they have to take the initiative to bear spiritual fruit."

"Did I read too much into this by suggesting that the existential life is cursed to wither and die and pass into the recycling bin of nature, as Gurdjieff believed? This is why I asked you in one of my spiritual healing sessions with you if Jesus also believed that man is not born with an immortal soul, because Gurdjieff called his teaching 'esoteric Christianity'? After all, Christ's teaching is all about spiritual rebirth, which would presuppose that man does not have an immortal soul. But you told me no, Jesus did not hold that point of view. How cannot man be part of the whole, you said; and the whole being the Creator, then man would have to be *ipso facto* immortal; and Christ's teaching was all about realizing our immortal nature. So, was I correct in saying that Jesus cursed the fig tree to point to the barren life of our existential life?"

"The short answer is yes."

"And now we come to the crunch, the theme that this book is pointing to—the great reconciliation which Jesus spells out in his most paradoxical saying: **"He that loveth his life shall lose it; and he that hateth his life in this world shall keep it unto life eternal"** (John

12: 25). This is the conscious death that the Sufis refer to when they speak of 'dying before dying,' and what Socrates referred to when he spoke of soul "gathering and collecting herself into herself,' which I have simply called the great reconciliation."

"You certainly have taken the mystery out of Christ's teaching, but you have a way to go yet before you bring this book to closure."

"I fear repeating myself."

"Yes, there is that danger. But your creative self always provides a new context for the reader to get a better picture of the secret way. This is the underlying theme of your story, and getting the reader to see that their own life is the way to the great reconciliation will be a great boon for them. Yes, death is the final frontier; but the death your story is leading to is the conscious death of the false self. That's what Tolstoy pointed to with 'The Death of Ivan Ilych.' Tolstoy saw the false nature of his existential life through Ivan Ilych, and this affected him deeply. Writing this story dropped the scales from Tolstoy's eyes, and he became intensely spiritual in the last few years of his life because he saw that living a lie was meaningless—"

"Barren, you mean?"

"Yes, barren like the fig tree that Jesus cursed."

"So what would be the moral of Jesus cursing the fig tree?"

"Reflect on this for a moment and tell me what you think."

"I think Jesus was telling us that the purpose of life is to bear the fruit of our own nature. At the risk of repeating myself, Rumi said it best: *"These leaves, our bodily personalities, seem identical, /but the globe of soul-fruit /we make, /each is elaborately unique."* We are all trees in the mystic garden of life, and we are all pre-destined to bear the fruit of our own 'elaborately unique' nature. That's what I think Jesus was telling us by cursing the fig tree, and until someone proves different I'm sticking to this story."

"You won't get any argument from me, my friend."

"And now I wait for serendipity to come calling?"

"Yes. In the meantime, check Socrates out. See what he has to say to Phaedrus. It might prove relevant to the great reconciliation..."

22. THE DIVINE MADNESS OF EROS

"For all of man's wants and needs, the soul still longs to be whole…"

My name was also Phaedrus in my past lifetime in ancient Greece. I was a student of Pythagoras and studied his secret teaching, but I may get back to this after I re-acquaint myself with Plato's *Phaedrus* that my Oracle suggested I explore to see what Socrates had to say that may be relevant to this dialectic on the great reconciliation…

Sitting on my front deck sipping raspberry flavored green tea, I read Plato's *Phaedrus* again after many years and was glad to be back in Socrates's company, listening to him reason his way to the truth of his inquiry, a dialectical skill that he called philosophical thinking; and I came away from this dialogue with the strongest impression of the great reconciliation in the myth that Socrates created to explain the inherent conflict in man's soul.

The subject of inquiry was love; specifically, the divine madness of Eros—erotic love conceived by Plato as a fundamental creative impulse having a sensual element, which in the *Phaedrus* dialogue is symbolized by the erotic love of an old man for a boy.

Homosexual love was common in ancient Greece, which shocked me when I first read Plato in my youth; but reading the *Phaedrus* today (the Gay Pride Parade in Toronto the other day, *July 3, 2016*, was graced with our Prime Minister Justin Trudeau's presence) made me smile at how slow our modern world is to embrace our differences; but that's neither here nor there for the intended purpose of this dialectic on self-reconciliation.

Socrates likens the soul to a chariot with two horses and a charioteer. The greatest good for the soul is to grow wings and fly through the heavens with the gods. And if the soul is strong and controls its horses it catches sight of such true ideas as Beauty and Self-Knowledge beyond the heavens. But because the souls of men

DEATH, THE FINAL FRONTIER

however all have a bad horse they will eventually fall back down to earth. Now, when the soul catches a glimpse of a beautiful boy on earth (which is to say, falls madly in love), it is reminded of the vision of Beauty that it saw in the heavens. The resulting yearning is called Eros, and the soul that can control such yearning will be granted the philosopher's boon—an early return to heaven after three thousand years instead of ten thousand years. That's the myth according to Socrates.

In essence, Socrates is saying that love inspires the soul; but if love is ruled by uncontrollable passion (the bad horse), it keeps the soul earthbound; and if love is ruled by reason (the good horse), it lifts soul to the heavens. That's the Socratic argument.

When Socrates likened our soul to a chariot with two horses and a charioteer, I was immediately drawn back to my past lifetime in medieval Persia. My name was Salaam, and I was a member of a secret Sufi sect called the Order of the White Tiger. I have no empirical evidence and cannot verify that there was such a sect, but this is what my past-life regression revealed to me. My lifetime as Salaam was so real that I cannot help but believe that it was me, and I need no empirical proof for having lived this life—if empirical proof could even be found, that is. Nonetheless, the point I want to make is that in this lifetime I failed to be initiated into the Order of the White Tiger because I failed to pass the test of initiation. I was given three chances to pass the test, and upon my third failure I was banished from the Order and ended up a beggar dying of malnutrition and out of my mind.

My lifetime as Salaam the Sufi was a very hard life because I was torn between what I called "the two stallions of my life." One stallion was my love for God, and the other stallion was my love for sex; and I could not tame my stallions. That's why the Socratic myth in the *Phaedrus* spoke to me and instantly brought back memories of my Sufi lifetime—and, I suspect, the reason why my Oracle wanted me to read the *Phaedrus* dialogue again.

My test of initiation for the Order of the White Tiger was to voluntarily control my "tiger of desire," which was an honor test. I had to go out into the world and live the Sufi life of controlling my "tiger of desire." And every three years I was called by the Order to see if I had passed the test. The third time I was called I had to answer that I could not control my "tiger of desire," and I was banished from the Order; and I brought that karmic baggage with me into my current lifetime, which was a burden I cannot begin to describe.

I did have one past lifetime after my Sufi life in which I abandoned completely to my "tiger of desire" just to have the experience of sexual abandon (for reasons which may be too esoteric for this book but which I explain in my novel *Cathedral of My Past Lives*), and that was my lifetime in Paris, France in the mid-17th Century. My name was Riel Laforchette, and I was known as *le Salaud de Paris,* which translated means *the Scoundrel of Paris*. I was given this name because I was morally and sexually debauched, and I mention this only to illustrate that we bring our karmic baggage with us every time we take on a new life. So not only did I have the unresolved karma of my lifetime as Salaam the Sufi to contend with in my present lifetime, but also all of that abandoned sexual passion that I had unleashed in my lifetime as *le Salaud de Paris*; this is why I had to find the secret way in my current life—because I had to save myself from myself!

Ironically, I had an inner knowledge of the secret way because of my lifetime in ancient Greece as a student of Pythagoras who taught in secret the sacred knowledge of self-reconciliation; that's why I've always had an affinity for ancient Greek philosophy, especially Socrates whose personal expression of the secret way spoke to me from the day I discovered Plato when I purchased an encyclopedic set of books called *The Great Books of the Western World* when I was fifteen years old. (I had to have my older brother sign the purchase order for me, but which I faithfully paid for every month for three or four years with after school and summer jobs.) But even though the secret way spoke to me, it wasn't until I started living Gurdjieff's teaching of "work on oneself" that I began to discern its purpose, which was to reconcile my lower and higher self—*the two stallions of my life!*

"So, are you happy now, Padre?"

"*Very much so. You have opened up the door to the biggest obstacle facing man on his journey of self-discovery, his desire and passion for life. This is the paradoxical dilemma that has to be resolved for man to realize the fruit of his nature, a dilemma that drives every soul to despair and obliges one to return to life again and again to find the way to liberation."*

"To which my own past lives can attest!"

"You are living proof of this dilemma. But would you please explain it for your reader. I fear it is still up in the air and much too abstract to pin down."

"The paradox is this: man needs the energy of life experience to grow into what he is meant to be, but like the teenager that needs more nutrition to feed its growing body so does man need more life experience to feed its growing self; this is where our passion for life comes from. The more energy we need to nourish the longing in our soul to be what we are meant to be, the more passion we have for life; but the paradox is that life cannot satisfy this longing in our soul to be whole, regardless how addicted we are to life—be it through sports, work, sex, the arts, travel, whatever. Our desire for life cannot satisfy our longing for wholeness and completeness. We need another source of energy to satisfy this longing, but where can we get this energy? This is man's dilemma."

"And the paradox is?"

"The paradox is that man must detach himself from his desires to satisfy his longing, which is next-to-impossible to do. I could not do it in my Sufi lifetime. I tried, but my tiger of desire always got the best of me. And that's the irony. We have to detach ourselves from our desires to obtain the energy that will satisfy this longing in our soul. As unfair as this may seem, it's the only way to satisfy our longing for wholeness and completeness; and had I not experienced the birth of my immortal self that day in my mother's kitchen which satisfied this longing in my soul (to this day I no longer suffer the pangs of longing to be me), I would seriously question this whole premise of the great reconciliation. But you know this, Padre; because you experienced the great reconciliation through your suffering of the stigmata, plus all of that extra 'glory' that you granted yourself through voluntary suffering. You knew the spiritual value of suffering; that's why you called it your glory. But how in God's name can one sell this path of suffering to the modern world? People want the good life, not a life of intentional suffering. People want to retire and play golf, go skiing, and hike and garden and take vacations to far-away places or whatever. This is the goal of life today. What's the point of this dialectic on self-reconciliation in today's modern world of self-indulgence?"

"For all of man's wants and needs, the soul still longs to be whole; and it doesn't matter how much time one spends on their existential life, they can never satisfy the longing of their essential nature. It takes a different kind of energy to satisfy this longing. One would be wrong to believe that this energy can only come from suffering. Suffering does not create this energy that man needs to satisfy his longing to be whole; suffering merely purifies the energy that one has already realized through life experience. This energy is man's karma. Suffering resolves one's karmic energies and nourishes one's longing to be whole; but this is not enough. Soul needs the energy that comes from unselfish living to satisfy its longing. This is how man can resolve his dilemma. He has to go against his primal selfish nature and stop taking from life and start giving back to life, because in the giving of oneself to life soul realizes its divine nature and satisfies its longing to be whole. This is the solution to man's dilemma. Become a volunteer. Be more generous with people. Start giving back to life instead of always taking from life. That's the simple answer, and why I said to you that life is a journey of the self. But every soul must learn this on its own, because as you have rightly pointed out there is only self-initiation into the central mystery of man's existence."

"I sense a certain impatience in your tone."

"Sometimes man is hard of hearing and one has to shout into his ear. Just keep in mind that there is more than one way to skin a cat."

"On that note, we can call it a day."

"I agree. Keep your eyes peeled for your next chapter. It will come to you from where you least expect it."

"Thus sayeth my Oracle!"

"Touché..."

23. MEMORIES AND THE SELF

"What a person believes in makes a difference in how they feel when they're faced with their own mortality..."

I don't know what this has to do with the great reconciliation, but I suspect that an experience I had yesterday afternoon (*Sunday, July 10, 2016*) when I went to Johnson's Market in Midland to pick up some freshly-picked southern Ontario corn was the opening that my Oracle said I should be on the lookout for to introduce this chapter, and I'm going to trust my creative instincts and just go with it...

When Penny and I moved from my hometown of Nipigon to Bluewater, Tiny Township in Georgian Bay thirteen years ago, I discovered Johnson's Market on Highway 93 going into the town of Midland, and I made acquaintances with the owner, a man by the name of Jimmy Johnson who once played hockey for the Marathon Mercuries in the North Shore Hockey League in Northwestern Ontario. The four towns in the league were Marathon, Terrace Bay, Nipigon, and Red Rock; and Jimmy Johnson knew all the players then.

The first time I went into Johnson's Market I noticed a picture of a hockey team on the back shelf wall, and upon closer inspection I saw that it was a picture of the Marathon Mercuries. I commented that I was from Nipigon and I used to watch the Mercuries when they played my hometown team, the Nipigon Flyers, and then Jimmy told me that he played for the Mercuries; that's when my memories came flooding back—

"I remember you," I said, excitedly. "You were a real scrapper, weren't you?"

Jimmy's eyes lit up, twinkling with a mischievous glint. "That was me," he said. "My nickname was Chicken Coop Johnson, and I got into a lot of scraps…"

And if Jimmy was behind the cash whenever I dropped into his market we would talk about the good old hockey days, which made his day.

I dropped into the market last Saturday for a basket of field tomatoes and asked Jimmy if he had any corn, and he told me he would have some on Sunday; so I dropped in Sunday with Penny and Jimmy asked me if some of the old players were still around, but sadly all the players he asked about had passed on.

Jimmy is eighty-four, but still looks fit and healthy for his age. In fact, he told me he was up at 3. A. M. Sunday morning and drove to Southern Ontario for the corn, so he's still going strong. I asked if Penny could take a picture of us together with him holding the picture of his Marathon Mercuries Hockey team so I could post it on Facebook. "Yeah, sure," he said, with big smile on his impish face.

When Penny and I left with our bag of freshly-picked corn, I said to her: "We just made Jimmy's day. Did you see his face light up?"

"What did he call you when you went in?"

"He called me the Nipigon Flash, but he usually calls me Kid and I call him Old Timer. I love talking with him. He comes alive when we talk about his hockey days. You know, sweetheart; life is about good memories. If we don't have good memories when we get old, life can get pretty lonely. Good memories nourish the soul."

But I didn't make the connection that my Oracle wanted me to make with my little trip down memory lane. I knew that my little talk with Jimmy was my opening to this chapter on death, the final frontier of life; but I couldn't see what connection it had with the great reconciliation. But taking my cue from my literary mentor Ernest Hemingway, rather than puzzle it out I forgot about it and let my creative unconscious work on it; and this morning, while making coffee, it came to me— *"my spiritual musing!"*

I saw the connection instantly. The memories that Jimmy Johnson and I stirred up on Sunday and his curiosity about whether some of the old players were still around brought to mind a spiritual musing I had written for my blog about memories and the self; but rather than explain what connection this has with the great reconciliation, I'll copy and paste my musing in its entirety, and then I can discuss it with my Oracle in the following chapter: —

To Be and Not to Be
Personal Identity and Alzheimer's

"We are more than the memory of who we are," I said to Penny on our drive home from the Uptown Theatre and early dinner in Barrie yesterday afternoon, and I knew instantly that this was my entry point into the spiritual musing that the movie *Still Alice* had inspired; and this morning I called upon my Muse to help me explore the haunting question of personal identity and Alzheimer's that the remarkable movie *Still Alice* inevitably gave rise to...

I didn't really want to see *Still Alice,* starring Julianne Moore who won an Oscar for her moving performance of the fifty-year old Alice Howland, professor of linguistics at Columbia University afflicted with early-onset Alzheimer's, because I knew it would be a tear jerker; but we went anyway, and it proved to be a three-tissue movie.

But it wasn't so much the emotional impact that Alice had upon me as Alzheimer's ravages her memory, even though that in itself easily moved me to tears; it was the unbearable irony of her tragic predicament: Alice is an exceptionally bright high-achiever whose personal identity is inextricably linked with her intellect, and when she loses her memory she loses her sense of self-identity and slowly sinks into an abyss of blank-faced dumbness from which she won't recover.

This bothered me more than her disease, not because I didn't empathize with Alice's rapid deterioration and the effect it had upon her loving family, but because this beautiful and gracious wife and mother of three responsible adult children was hopelessly trapped by the spiritually suffocating scientific constraints of her condition; and with each passing day and hour and minute her comfortable middle-class world slowly shrank into memory-fading oblivion.

"You know, sweetheart," I said to Penny as we drove through Minesing on our way home to Bluewater in Georgian Bay after the heartbreaking movie and simple hot hamburger dinner at Wimpy's Diner, "what a person believes in makes a difference in how they feel when they're faced with their own mortality, or a tragic disease like Alice in the movie. Do you remember me telling you about my buddy Michael Ignatieff's novel *Scar Tissue* that dealt with this same issue of Alzheimer's and personal identity?"

"Vaguely," Penny said. "But you're going to remind me, aren't you?"

I was being sarcastic when I called the disgraced former leader of the Liberal Party of Canada Michael Ignatieff my buddy, because I had lost respect for him when he forced a totally unnecessary election that decimated the Liberal Party and reduced it to third party status. "Those who can't, teach," I responded to his catastrophic and personally humiliating defeat (he even lost his own Toronto's Etobicoke-Lakeshore seat) when he resigned as leader of the Official Opposition and ignominiously shrunk away with his bushy academic tail between his legs to teach at the University of Toronto and then back to Harvard's ivory tower where he had been plucked by the Liberal Party establishment as the next Pierre Trudeau to save Canada from Premier Stephen Harper and the Conservative Party.

I respected former professor/journalist/author Michael Ignatieff, whose TV show *Ignatieff* I watched with avid interest (I distinctly remember his interview with Hemingway's third wife Martha Gellhorn, whose life with Hemingway inspired the movie *Hemingway and Gellhorn* which in turn inspired my book *The Lion that Swallowed Hemingway*, and I read with fascination Ignatieff's autobiographical novel *Scar Tissue* that was shortlisted for the Booker Prize because the core of his story was about Alzheimer's and personal identity, just as the movie *Still*

Alice that was based on the *New York Times* bestselling novel by neuroscientist Lisa Genova.

I didn't lose respect for Ignatieff because he aspired to become Prime Minister of Canada, which is a noble if not impossible ambition for even the most astute politician; but because it was an arrogant presumption to think that he could squirm his way to the top position of the Liberal Party and become Prime Minister without paying his political dues, which was why he was branded by the Conservative Party attack adds during the ill-timed election as "arrogant and elitist," and it wasn't by any stretch of imagination that I connected the dots of his massive ego with his novel *Scar Tissue* whose theme was so intimate and personal that it caused a rift with his family, especially with his brother Andrew who was primary caregiver for his mother and not Michael as he wrote in *Scar Tissue*.

Michael Ignatieff's mother fell prey to Alzheimer's, and he watched her lose her sense of self as her memory faded from week to week until she mercifully passed away in a nursing home; and his novel explored the theme of loss of memory and self-identity, because the narrator of *Scar Tissue* is a philosophy professor not unlike the author who is haunted by his fear of inheriting his mother's Alzheimer's, and what better way for the professor-turned-politician, who when campaigning for the leadership of the Liberal Party of Canada cleverly called himself "neither atheist nor believer," to immortalize his name than to become Prime Minster of Canada just in case Alzheimer's erased his memory? What better confirmation could one have to validate their insecure egoic need to *be*?

I have no doubt that in his mind the Harvard professor's motives for entering Canadian politics were pure and altruistic (despite the fact that he lived outside Canada for thirty years, he professed to a philosophy of *engagement* to justify his commitment to the Liberal Party), but novels based on one's personal life have a tendency to reveal much more than the author realizes, as many writers have learned after a critical study of their work; and Michael Ignatieff's intensely personal and poignant novel *Scar Tissue* reflected the tremulous shadow side of the author's scholarly trained ego that goes straight to the issue of consciousness and individual identity: **is our reflective self-consciousness an epiphenomenon of our biology, which disappears when our body dies; or does our reflective self co-exist with our physical body and continues to exist non-biologically after our body dies?**

This is the core issue of *Scar Tissue* that Michael Ignatieff tried to come to terms with creatively through narrative inquiry, and it is the same issue in the movie *Still Alice* that is left hanging in the air as Alice fades away into herself, and it also happens to be the issue that I devoted my whole life to resolving and writing about in my novels, essays, and memoirs and which is the premise of today's musing. Having said this, I can now proceed to the heart of the issue of being *and* not being who we are...

Alzheimer's is like a magnifying glass, focusing our attention on the individual self; because as one loses one's memory with the ravages of this disease, one's self-identity disappears. But where does it go? That's the heart of the issue.

Science would have us believe that when we die, the matrix of consciousness that makes up our self-identity dies with us; or, generously speaking, science may allow the possibility that like energy which can neither be created nor destroyed but simply changes form, the matrix of our reflective self-consciousness may simply go back into the cosmic stream of life, which is what the Buddhist philosophy contends.

Ignatieff's inquiry into the issue of Alzheimer's and self-identity appears to hold this point of view. Bringing his narrative to closure, the author/narrator says: "But I know that there is a life beyond this death, a time beyond this time. I know that at the very last moment, when everything I ever knew has been effaced from my mind, when pure vacancy has taken possession of me, then light of the purest whiteness will stream in through my eyes into the radiant and empty plain of my mind."

But this is the non-self of the Buddhist philosophy; not the individuated consciousness of our autonomous self that pre-exists our physical body and continues to exist when our body dies.

I've already explored this issue in my book *Stupidity Is Not a Gift of God* in my essay "On the Evolutionary Impulse to Individuate: A Response to the Spiritual Path of Evolutionary Enlightenment," so I need not go into detail here; suffice to say that in my quest for resolution to the issue of the self, I came to the conclusion that we are all born with a spark of divine consciousness that evolves through life into an individual and autonomous self; and the self evolves naturally through the karmic process of being and becoming. To *be*, we have to *become*; and we *become* who we are according to how we live our life. That's the central mystery of the human condition that I have explored in my book *The Pearl of Great Price*

Given my personal perspective, then; I see the matrix of consciousness that we call our reflective self not as a byproduct (epiphenomenon) of the brain (our neurology), but as an autonomous self that exists independently of our body; but what other proof do we have?

In the movie *Still Alice*, Alice Howland loses her self-identity as her memory is erased by early-onset Alzheimer's; but was her self-identity a byproduct of her neurological system which disappears into oblivion when that part of her brain is ravaged by her disease, or does it recede elsewhere where it cannot be seen?

In other words, is Alice *still* Alice despite the loss of her memory of who she is? Would Alice *still* be Alice if she lost a leg, an arm, a breast, or a vital organ that had to be replaced, like her heart?

Many heart transplant patients have reported the phenomenon of taking on personality traits of their donors, like Jane Seymour did in the movie *Heart of a Stranger* that was inspired by the true story of Claire Sylvia's heart transplant; but that's a separate musing that I hope to write one day. The point of today's spiritual musing is this: is our self-identity limited to our memory alone, or does it pervade throughout the cells of our entire body as pioneer researcher in cellular consciousness Dr. Graham Farrant and Dr. Paul Pearlsall (*The Heart's Code*) have discovered, and even beyond cellular memory in non-biological form after our body dies? And if so, what proof do we have besides my own conviction?

In October, 2012 Dr. Eben Alexander, a practicing neurosurgeon for twenty-five years who was scientifically convinced that self-identity was an epiphenomenon of the brain, had a unique if not providentially inspired medical experience that changed his entire scientific perspective on consciousness and made him a believer in the independent existence of our individual and autonomous self, and he wrote a book on the experience that initiated him into the divine mystery of the self. The book is called *Proof of Heaven, A Neurosurgeon's Journey into the Afterlife*; and it was on the New York Times bestseller list for 97 weeks.

"On November 10, 2008," he wrote in his book, "I was struck by a rare illness and thrown into a coma for seven days. During that time, my entire neocortex—the outer surface of the brain, the part that makes us human—was shut down. Inoperative. In essence, absent." Dr. Alexander believed that "the brain is a machine that produces consciousness," and when "the machine breaks down, consciousness stops." But the rare illness that he contracted (which proved to be a rare virus) shut his brain down and sent him into a seven-day coma that should have shut his consciousness down according to his scientific paradigm, but Dr. Alexander instead experienced himself outside his body in what Dr. Raymond Moody (*Life After Life*) described as the most astounding near-death experiences that he had studied in more than four decades of researching the incredible phenomenon of near death experiences.

In the Prologue to *Proof of Heaven*, former non-believer Dr. Alexander contritely wrote: "My experience showed me that the death of the body and the brain are not the end of consciousness, that human experience continues beyond the grave. More important, it continues under the gaze of God who loves and cares about each one of us and about where the universe itself and all the beings within it are ultimately going," which means, quite simply, that Alice was *still* Alice despite her loss of memory!

I wrote this spiritual musing because the movie got under my skin. Alice, her family, and the whole scientific community were so stuck in the existential dimension of life that I had to offer a spiritual perspective; but how much proof do we need to convince ourselves that we are more than our physical body? That's the question of the day, and the inspiration for my next chapter…

24. HOW MUCH PROOF DO WE NEED?

"Death does not negate the self..."

"I didn't expect that, Padre. Was this your way of letting the reader know that our self-identity is more than the memories of our existential life?"

"I knew you would make the connection. Loss of memory is a biological experience and has nothing to do with one's essential self. That's the point I wanted you to get across to your reader, because most people can't make the connection that you made in your spiritual musing. The existential self may forget who it is, like Alice in the movie; but the essential self never forgets who it is, because soul is the individuated consciousness of its existential self that continues to exist after the physical body dies. Nice work, my friend."

"Thank you. But I suspect you planted the seed this morning while I was making coffee. The thought just came to me out of the blue, and I know that when an idea or insight just comes to me it has been planted by *the omniscient guiding principle of life*. Or maybe it just bubbled up from my creative unconscious because of my talk with Jimmy Johnson on Sunday. Many writers have learned to let their creative unconscious work out the impasses in their writing, so was it my unconscious that made the connection of memory and the self?"

*"Again, what does it matter where it came from? Call it your creative unconscious, God, the omniscient guiding principle of life, Divine Spirit, your Higher Self or Padre Pio; it does not matter, because these are all names for the I Am consciousness of the Creator. What you were meant to learn from this experience was to connect memory with the I Am consciousness of the self, which cannot be erased by a disease like Alzheimer's or disappear when the body dies. I cannot stress this enough: **death does not negate the self.**"*

"On another note—or maybe it's not another note, just another one of those little digressions that will expand upon the theme of our dialectic on death, the final frontier of life—I had an interesting little encounter with a couple of Jehovah's Witnesses yesterday while I was on my front deck reading. I remember from reading all those biographies of your life that you weren't fond of the Jehovah's Witnesses, nor the Masons or women with short dresses for that matter, if you don't mind my bluntness, and this experience inspired a poem that I'd like to share with you because it speaks to something I feel needs to be explored to expand upon the reader's understanding on the issue of man's becoming. What I'm trying to say Padre, is that our beliefs contain us; and if our beliefs will not allow us to grow, how can we realize our destined purpose? Would you like to hear my poem?"

"*By all means.*"

"Alright. I wrote it shortly after the Jehovah's Witnesses left. I wanted to capture the moment, which is what all good poetry seeks to do; but because I've learned to let the creative spirit of my unconscious guide my poetry, something came out of this poem that I did not expect, and I'd like to hear what you have to say about it. Here's my poem: —

Jehovah's Witnesses at My Door

Dick and Mary ("Not Dick and Jane," he said)
came to my door this morning (I was sitting
on the deck reading WRITING IN GENERAL AND
THE SHORT STORY IN PARTICULAR,), Jehovah's
Witnesses, a lovely couple about to celebrate
their 60th wedding anniversary, a long time to
be together, and Mary had the loveliest smile
(which I made a point of telling her) and Dick
as content as could be in their missionary zeal,
and I listened, not out of courtesy but out of
respect for their age and commitment, and we
talked for twenty minutes about the end of times
and free will (I championed free will, they the
Bible) and world events and other things, but
mostly sticking to their closed script, and when
they left smiling at their surprising reception I
read their two WATCHTOWER pamphlets ("Has

Science Replaced the Bible" and "Your Cells Living Libraries!") and opened the book that Dick wanted me to read, WHAT DOES THE BIBLE REALLY TEACH? and started reading, not that I was thinking of converting, but because I told Dick and Mary I would read it, but nineteen pages into the glossy little book and I had to put it aside because it was too hard to swallow; nice people Dick and Mary, but an absurd religion.

"There you have it, Padre. As convinced as I am about the absurdity of the Jehovah's Witnesses religion, which is too bizarre to get into here, I can't deny the goodness that I saw in Dick and Mary. Those are their real names, by the way. But wasn't this how I opened up our dialogue in my spiritual healing sessions with you for my novel *Healing with Padre Pio*? I wanted you to confirm my perception of the Christian religion, how I felt that it inhibited spiritual growth because its core beliefs were ill-founded, like the belief that soul is created at the moment of human conception, that we only live one lifetime, and that hell is a place of eternal damnation. I felt that these beliefs kept soul stuck on one level of consciousness. But then you told me something that opened me up to a whole new perspective on our becoming; you said that life was all about GROWTH and UNDERSTANDING. It didn't' matter what path one was on, the purpose of one's path was growth and understanding. Isn't that what you said?"

"I did. And despite what I thought about the Jehovah's Witnesses back in my lifetime in San Giovanni Rotondo, the same can be said about this religion. It serves its purpose to give its followers the experiences they need for their individual growth. If this is the experience that these souls chose to have in their incarnation, then who are we to question the wisdom of the Divine Plan of God? As I said, life is all about growth and understanding, and it doesn't matter what path one is on because they all serve the Divine Purpose."

"And if you would, please define this Divine Purpose?"

"To individuate the I Am consciousness of God."

"I understand. But this is where I get my back up with so many teachings, especially the New Age Religion that I lived for over thirty years. I know that you told me I needed that experience to get to where I am today, but even so I can't help but feel that there's something wrong with this picture. As much as I agree with you that life is all about growth and understanding, surely one doesn't have to suffer the indignity of being made a fool of by such outrageous teachings as the Jehovah's Witnesses and that New Age Religion?"

"You can't let it go, can you?"

"No, I can't. It's not nice, playing us for fools. Was the whole point of my experience (as Dick and Mary's) to consolidate my vanity to the point where I had no more room for growth and understanding, as I felt happened to me in my New Age Religion? I had to leave because I could not stomach the vanity that I saw in my spiritual community. I didn't see any growth in my fellow chelas. All I saw was insufferable spiritual conceit. That's why I had to leave. And I have you to thank for that, because my experience with you in my spiritual healing sessions with the psychic medium who channeled you gave me the confidence to step away from that teaching. And as much as I don't want to say it, I saw this same insufferable spiritual conceit in Dick and Mary yesterday as they stuck to their sacred script. Are they still growing in their religion, or have they ossified in their outrageous beliefs?"

"I have to grant it to you, my friend. Yes, Dick and Mary have ossified in their beliefs and have to see their path to the end of this incarnation. But as you said, essentially they are good people. They're just confused, that's all. But aren't we all in one way or another? Name one person free of life's confusion and I will bow down and worship them."

"How about Jesus Christ?"

"What a joy you are, my friend! Do you have any more concerns?"

"No. I think that about covers it for this chapter. And since it makes no difference what I call my inspiration, do you have any suggestions for my next chapter?"

"As a matter of fact, I do. Concentrate on giving..."

25. THE IRONY OF OUR BECOMING

"There is only so much that can be said on the sacred knowledge of the secret way..."

When I began this book I had no idea where my thoughts on death would take me, but along the way I began to see a light at the end of my creative tunnel; and now I'm convinced that the whole point of this book was to bring the reader to a place where they can see the irony of our becoming, because not until we learn how to resolve the paradox of our *being* (essential self) and *non-being* (existential self) will we fulfill our destined purpose which my Oracle implied by pointing to the great reconciliation through the virtue of giving.

But before I abandon to my creative unconscious to explore the virtue of giving, let me explain what I mean by the irony of our becoming. This is the greatest irony that we will ever experience because it will be such a shock to our system, but it cannot be avoided on our destined journey to wholeness and completeness: **we have to die to our life to realize our life.**

That's the irony of our becoming, and not until we resolve the paradoxical nature of our *being* and *non-being* will we become what we are meant to be...

We are all on various stages on our journey to wholeness and completeness, a journey that we are all pre-destined to realize despite what we may believe; and when we are ready to move on to the next stage of our journey but are unwilling to embrace the new challenge, life will come calling with an experience to jolt us out of our complacency.

Psychologist Teresa DeCicco explores this phenomenon in her insightful book *Living Beyond the Five Senses, The Emergence of a Spiritual Being*. "Ultimately, we see that some people are at one end of the continuum of *Homo nouvo* where the world is only material and perceived through the five senses. At the other end are those who are completely transformed into Spiritual Beings, but most will be somewhere in the middle," she writes, reflecting the reality of the various stages of our becoming from the exoteric circle of life through the mesoteric and eventually to the esoteric where the Spiritual Being is centered; but getting to this place of wholeness and completeness cannot be done without help from *the omniscient guiding principle of life*. This is the mystery of our becoming.

As we grow through the exoteric stage of our becoming we begin to sense that there is more to life than material existence, which Teresa DeCicco confirms in the same chapter ("Mental Modifications"): "Most people will have a flicker of awareness at some point in their lives that life on this planet is more than mere survival and material gain. When this happens for each individual is unknown and it appears that it cannot be forced. Some have to experience crisis after crisis and much suffering before the mind will open to a new way of being. For others it may happen in an instant; one comment from a stranger, one glance from a homeless person, one word, and the realization is made that humans are in this experience for a higher purpose," and this higher purpose is to realize the destined purpose of our divine nature, what psychologist Teresa DeCicco calls *Homo nuovo*.

In one of my favorite books on C. G. Jung, *Jung and the Story of Our Time,* Laurens van der Post reveals what I've come to believe to be Jung's breakthrough insight into the mystery of our becoming while working as a young psychiatrist at the Burgholzli Mental Hospital in Zurich. With disciplined patience and compassion, Dr. Jung listened to his patients and tried to make sense of their incomprehensible glossolalia, but one day it dawned on him that all of his patients had a story, a myth of their own to unfold, and the reason they were in the mental hospital was because their story got interrupted (by a traumatic shock to the mind), and it was his goal to get hold of the person's story and help them get unstuck from their mental impasse so they could continue living the story of their life.

"Jung said that he learned from the start how in every disturbance of the personality," wrote Laurens van der Post in his memoir, "even in the most extreme psychotic form of schizophrenia, one could discern the elements of a personal story. The story was the personality's most precious possession, whether it knew that or not, and the person could only be cured, or healed by the psychiatrist getting hold of the story. That was the secret key to unlock the door which barred reality in all its dimensions within and without from entering the personality and transforming it" (*Jung and the Story of Our Time,* p. 119).

Every person's life is a story unique to the individual, but as original as our life stories may be we are all pre-destined to realize our divine nature, and for all of our diversity we are all the same in our destined purpose of self-realization consciousness.

"Life is a journey of the self," said St. Padre Pio, and my own past-life regressions confirm my own journey from the Body of God where we all come from as atoms of God (embryonic souls without self-consciousness) to my first primordial human lifetime where I gave birth to my reflective self-consciousness, and on up to my current lifetime where I took evolution into my own hands with the sacred knowledge of the secret way to complete the rest of my journey to wholeness and completeness; so I'm intimately familiar with the stages of our becoming, which Jung called the *process of individuation*, and I can "see" these stages of our becoming in every person's story. This is why I love poetry.

The poet has the gift of intuitive insight into the secret way of life, though most poets don't know it, and every poem that they write shines a light upon the process of our becoming; which is why I had to write a poem in praise of the poet's imperative: —

Ode to the Poet

"God," said I, "be my help and stay secure;
I'll think of the Leech Gatherer on the
lonely moor!" wrote Wordsworth,
lighting my soul on fire, —

Every poet explores their own stage
on this journey through life, not yours
or mine, but their own rendition of
the messy human condition, —

But not unlike yours or mine, the poet
speaks to every soul, and we look to
poetry to confirm our own place
in the cosmic journey, —

Some poets are obscure, some recondite;
but esoteric or mesoteric, every poem
administers one more truth to heal
our soul and set us free from the
ennui of our lonely journey.

Poetry can set people free from the ruts of their life, but poetry is not the only medium that speaks the language of the secret way; so does art, music, creative writing, theatre and movies—not to mention dreaming, which speaks the silent language of the secret way with symbolic genius. In one of his trans readings, America's greatest psychic Edgar Cayce said that dreams "work to accomplish two things. They work to solve the problems of the dreamer's conscious, waking life. And they work to quicken in the dreamer new potentials which are his to claim" (*Edgar Cayce On Dreams*, by Harmon H. Bro, PhD with Hugh Lynn Cayce, p. 16). This is the divine imperative of the secret way—*to help every soul realize its destined purpose;* and it speaks to us with every experience we have throughout the day.

But can we see it? Can we hear it? This puzzled Christ's Disciples. They asked Jesus why he spoke to public in parables, and he replied: ***"Because it is given unto you to know the mysteries of the kingdom of heaven, but to them it is not given. For whosoever hath, to him shall be given, and he shall have more abundance; but whosoever hath not, from him shall be taken away even that he hath"*** (Matthew 13: 11-12).

Jesus is speaking in code—the metaphorical language of the secret way. And he's telling his Disciples that one has to be made ready by life to be given the sacred knowledge of the secret way which will open the door to the kingdom of heaven; meaning, the key to *conscious evolution* which will fulfill soul's destined purpose.

"Many are called, but few are chosen," said Jesus in another parable (Matthew 22: 2-14, the marriage of the king's son), reaffirming that one has to be made ready by life to "see" and "hear" the silent language of the secret way, and had I not experienced this when I "worked" on myself with Gurdjieff's teaching and my *Royal Dictum* I would have trouble believing that life speaks to us in a silent language to guide us in our journey through life; but I did experience it, and whether one believes this or not does not matter to me, because I've long ago realized that there is only self-initiation into the mysteries of life and not until one is ready will they be called to live the secret way consciously. And with this, I can now get on with the virtue of giving; but not without consulting my Oracle first…

"Padre, I think I've covered everything that had to be said to shine a light upon one's journey to wholeness and completeness, but before I expound upon the virtue of giving (it feels like I'm about to bring this book to closure) I'd like to ask if you have anything to add to my perspective on the process of individuation."

"There is only so much that can be said on the sacred knowledge of the secret way, because it has to be lived to be understood. As you expressed it in one of your books, 'The more you live the Way, the more the Way reveals itself to you.' This is the paradox of the Way. It's the same old cliché: you can lead a horse to water, but you can't make it drink. I'm content with what we have done so far, but we have a few more things to discuss before we bring this book to closure."

"I guess I'm just anxious to get to my other writing. I should know better than to rush a book. Books are like people; they have their own part to play on the stage of life, and they know when it's time to exit stage left."

"Well said. There is one thing I would add to your perspective on the individuation process, and that would be to let the reader decide for themselves which path to take on their journey to their destined purpose. Let one's guide be Frost's poem 'The Road Not Taken.' Robert Frost wanted to be a poet, and he took the road less travelled by; and that made all the difference to his life. Every person will be brought to a crossroads in their life, not once but many times because God is merciful; so one need not worry if they do not take the road that will challenge them to grow in consciousness—"

"Pardon my interruption! That's what I wanted to discuss with you—the reason why Jesus spoke to the public in parables! Please, explain why Jesus did that. His Disciples were ready to hear the sacred knowledge of the secret way, but the public wasn't; why?"

"You have made this amply clear. But if you would like me to amplify I would be happy to comply. What is life for if not for growth? And what is growth for if not for the realization of life's inherent potential, which is the I Am consciousness of God. But if I may, what lesson did you learn from writing your spiritual musings?"

"I learned many lessons. But my final lesson was the realization that one can only pour so much tea into a cup. Pour too much and the tea spills over the rim. When I wrote my last musing *'Horizontal & Vertical Literature'* I knew I had poured all the tea that my reader's cup could hold, and I had to move on to another format to give expression to my creative impulse, which I'm doing by writing poetry and short stories. But what's your point?"

"My point is the same point that Jesus tried to make with his Disciples. Let a person's consciousness be one's tea cup. The size of one's cup determines how much sacred knowledge they can receive. Life made Christ's Disciples ready to receive the sacred knowledge of the secret way, because they had grown enough in consciousness to contain it; but the public had to be given the sacred knowledge in parables and sayings because a direct expression of the sacred knowledge would have been too much for them and would only have spilled over and wasted. Jesus made this point in the extreme when he admonished his Disciples to not cast pearls before swine. But there was a deeper reason why he said this. Why don't you look up the saying and we can reveal the real reason why Jesus had to speak in parable to the public."

"Give me a moment…Here it is, Matthew, Chapter 7, Verse 6: **"Give not that which is holy unto the dogs, neither cast ye pearls before swine, lest they trample them under their feet, and turn again and rend you."** As much as I hate to say this Padre, because I know it may come back to bite me; but that's exactly how I felt about my spiritual musings. I don't want to say that it felt like I was casting pearls before swine, but it sure felt like it. The best I can do to explain why I had to stop writing my spiritual musings for my blog was that I felt I was giving something holy to my readers and it was being wasted. I had brought my readers to the surfeit of their consciousness and the sacred knowledge of my spiritual musings was having an opposite effect. This is not unlike the realization I had a long time ago when I practiced the virtue of giving. I came to the shocking realization that people can only tolerate so much goodness in a person before they turn on him because goodness makes people conscious of their selfish nature, and people don't want to see how selfish they really are. Too much goodness threatens people, and so does the sacred knowledge. That's why I had to stop writing my spiritual musings for my blog; rather than appreciate the sacred knowledge of the secret way, I sensed that they felt threatened. That's why Jesus admonished his Disciples to be as gentle as doves and wise as serpents when they gave his message to the world."

"Well said. This was the lesson of my lifetime also."

"I know! I read the story of your life and how you were hounded! Was that why I was drawn to you, Padre? Was it because I resonated with you on some level that no one else seemed to understand? I know that too much goodness can turn people off; was that why we were meant to work together for my novel *Healing with Padre Pio?*"

"Yes, among other things. Does this answer your query?"

"I believe it does. So I guess my next chapter's going to be on the virtue of giving, seeing that we've loaded all the bases now."

"Your instincts may be right, my friend; you may very well bring your book home with the winning run in the virtue of giving."

"What a game this life is, Padre; what a game!"

26. THE WINNING RUN

*"There is an inborn dynamic process
that unites opposite positions within the psyche..."*

    I could not have asked for a neater way (pun intended on "way") to bring my thoughts on death, the final frontier of life to closure than to sum up my personal perspective on the process of individuation with a baseball metaphor, because **the virtue of giving is without doubt the winning run in the ball game of life,** and I'll tell you why. But before I do, let me share a curious little coincidence that speaks to the genius of the creative process...

    Yesterday I was strongly nudged to read *The Undiscovered Self,* by C. G. Jung, which I've read three or four times already; but I don't argue with my inner guidance when I'm nudged to read a book because I know it wants to tell me something that I need to know for the book that I'm working on, and it's never let me down yet. But I didn't make the connection until I engaged my Oracle in my last chapter and my creative unconscious surprised me with the symbol that's going to bring this dialectic to resolution—*the winning run in the virtue of giving.* I could not have thought of a better way to tie up all the loose ends than with the dynamic of the selfless self that the virtue of giving realizes, because this is the only way to complete what nature cannot finish and fulfill our destined purpose.

    "One cannot *invent* symbols," said Jung in *The Undiscovered Self;* "wherever they occur, they have not been devised by conscious intention and willful selection, because if such a procedure had been used, they would have been nothing but signs and abbreviations of conscious thought. Symbols occur to us spontaneously, as one can see in our dreams, which are not invented but which happen to us."

    The symbol of the winning run in the virtue of giving that brings closure to this book *happened* to me in my discourse with my Oracle (the spirit of St. Padre Pio or my creative unconscious, I really can't say); I did not invent it. It *happened* of its own accord, because this is what my book needed to bring this dialectic on the final frontier of life to happy resolution. This is how the transcendent function of the creative process works to bring natural resolution to the dual consciousness of our existential self and essential self—the *being* and *non-being* of our nature. Carl Jung realized this, which became the central motif of his psychology of individuation. In her introduction to *Encountering Jung: Jung on Active Imagination*, editor Joan Chodorow writes:

"His early concept of the transcendent function arose out of his attempts to understand how to come to terms with the unconscious. He found that there is an inborn dynamic process that unites opposite positions within the psyche. It draws polarized energies into a common channel, resulting in a new symbolic position which contains both perspectives. 'Either/or' choices become 'both/and,' but in a new and unexpected way. The transcendent function facilitates the transition from one attitude to another. Jung described it as 'a movement out of the suspension between two opposites, **a living birth that leads to a new level of being**, a new situation. Another time he defined it simply as 'the function of mediation between two opposites" (*Encountering Jung,* edited by Joan Chodorow, pp. 4-50, Bold italics mine).

But—*and this has to be the biggest* BUT *in the psychology of our becoming!* —the process of resolution through the natural mediation process of our unconscious can only take us so far on our destined journey to wholeness and completeness; to complete the journey we have to take evolution into our own hands, as I did when I took up Gurdjieff's teaching of "work on oneself." And I succeeded in my efforts to unite the dual consciousness of my *being* and *non-being*, which I expressed in the most dynamic statement of my entire life— **"I am what I am not, and I am not what I am; I am both but neither: I am Soul."**

This miraculous experience *happened* in my mother's kitchen one summer afternoon while she was kneading bread dough on the kitchen table. When it *happened*, I did not recognize it for the miraculous experience that it was, that came much later; all I remember of my experience is that in one surprising moment I *knew* that I was immortal.

There I was, talking with my mother when this feeling came over me and I *knew* that I was immortal and would never die; and from that moment almost forty years ago when I shifted my I-consciousness from my existential self to my essential self I have never once doubted my immortal nature or ever felt lonely again. I cannot describe this feeling of personal resolution any other way than to simply say: *in that moment I became what I was meant to be, whole and completely myself!*

This confirmed Christ's teaching of making the two into one, which is why I have the audacity to speak of our becoming with absolute certainty and conviction; and it is from my own journey of self-discovery that I can confidently say that not until we take evolution into our own hands will we realize our destined purpose; but—*and here again we have another big BUT that changes the whole dynamic of this bleak perspective that nature can only evolve us so far and no further!*—the dialectic of this book has given birth to the perspective of personal resolution with the winning run in the virtue of giving, because through the act of giving we can resolve the dual consciousness of our nature and transcend ourselves naturally; but I have to consult with my Oracle before I continue, because I cannot contain the excitement of the symbolic resolution that my creative unconscious has given birth to...

"Padre, is it possible? Can the biggest dilemma of man's existence be resolved with the virtue of giving? The thought is too much to bear. I spent years 'working' on myself to gather and collect myself into myself, if I may borrow the concept from Socrates—or better still, as St. Paul expressed it, 'dying daily' to realize my transcendent self, and now my creative unconscious tells me that the virtue of giving will accomplish the same goal of spiritual self-realization consciousness? Is this how man can escape through the horns of his dilemma?"

"*One never knows how Divine Spirit will respond to man's needs. Yes, man must die to his false nature to realize his higher self; but there is another kind of death besides the death of abstraction from one's lower nature. One can die to one's lower nature by growing in one's higher nature through the virtue of giving. This is the natural way to personal resolution that compliments the ancient teaching that nature can only evolve man so far and no further. The natural process of karma and reincarnation evolves man slowly but surely, and in the course of time man will be naturally inclined to serve life because this is what man needs to satisfy the longing in his soul to be all that he is meant to be. Pay close attention to your daily life. You will find the proof you need that the virtue of giving is born of the natural process of living and not the forced growth of conscious effort and intentional suffering as you experienced in your own journey of self-discovery."*

"Now you've really piqued my curiosity! Are you telling me that you can see the coincidence that will put this all together for me?"

"Let's just say that I trust God."

"So you don't know specifically what I'm going to experience that will confirm the natural law of spiritual resolution through giving, but you know I will experience it?"

"Yes."

"How can you know that I will experience it without knowing what I will experience? That doesn't make sense to me."

"You have free will, and what you experience depends upon your free will. You freely chose to explore your thoughts on the final frontier of life, and your creative unconscious has opened you up to the redemptive love of Divine Spirit; this is how I know that you will be given an experience to confirm the dialectical resolution of your story."

"So you don't know what exactly I will experience because that depends upon my own free will, but you know that I will experience something that will confirm the inherent logic of this story's dialectic—which is? Let's spell out this logic first, shall we?"

"The dialectic of your story has given birth to the symbol of the winning run in the ball game of life. This symbol speaks to the virtue of giving. By practicing the virtue of giving man tempers his selfish nature and grows in his divine nature. This is the natural way to resolve man's dilemma of having to die to one's life to save one's life, as Jesus expressed it. Instead of dying to one's life to save one's life, by practicing the virtue of giving one grows in one's divine

nature at the expense of one's lower self without all of that conscious effort to die to one's lower, selfish nature. This is where the dialectic of your story has brought you to, and all I am saying is that life will confirm this for you. So keep your eyes peeled, because the merciful law of divine synchronicity will come to your assistance with the ideal experience of naturally born altruism. This is the empirical proof you need to bring closure to your story."

"And you know this, why?"

"Because I trust God, my friend. I trust God..."

Sure enough, there it was two days later, in one of my weekend papers, the *Saturday July 16, 2016 Toronto Star*, under the headline banner "Using your skill set to give back," an article about retired Ontario Supreme Court Judge Sandra Chapnik whose life logic naturally inclined her to volunteer her time in the service of the human community!

I couldn't believe the remarkable coincidence, but I had to; and I read the article with avid interest just to see if the dialectic of my story was sound: ***life evolves us to the point where the only way we can satisfy the longing in our soul for wholeness and completeness is by practicing the virtue of giving.*** If she hadn't said it in her own words, I wouldn't have believed it; but here's the lead and second paragraph of the article in the *Toronto Star*: —

"Sandra Chapnik recently retired after more than 24 years as an Ontario Superior Court Judge, but she has no intention of retiring from involvement in the community. ***'It has always been important to me to give back,'*** Chapnik said. ***'Being involved in community service is part of who I always wanted to be and part of who I still am.'"*** And the article goes on to further confirm that life makes one ready to fulfil their destined purpose: "That's why throughout her career—from teacher to lawyer to judge—Chapnik has always volunteered her time. But now that she has more time on her hands, Chapnik said she's 'filling in the blanks, trying to find the causes that mean the most to me and that I can bring the most to" (*Toronto Star, Saturday, July 16, 2016,* by Jacqueline Kovacs, Bold italics mine).

Now I know for certain that synchronicities *happen* for a reason. But I know the virtue of giving well, because I know from personal experience in my own journey to resolution that this virtue would nourish the longing in one's soul for wholeness and completeness.

I practiced the virtue of giving as a conscious technique to enhance my spiritual growth when I realized that Gurdjieff's teaching of "work on oneself" needed an extra push to get me to my destined purpose, and for five summers I volunteered my time to Habitat for Humanity in Thunder Bay with my drywall taping skills, also texturing ceilings and painting. (I wrote my novel *On the Wings of Habitat* based on this experience.) But the horizons of the virtue of giving are wide and deep, and I grew in goodness exponentially with every act of charity that I did. I can't count the number of hitchhikers that I picked up and helped out with pocket money, and picking blueberries for some of my elderly painting customers, and other acts of charity; that's when I began to see the effect that goodness can have on people.

Just as people have a natural resistance to understanding as Jung realized, so do people have a natural resistance to a level of goodness beyond their endurance; and I had to learn how to be discreet in the virtue of giving....

"What do you have to say to that, Padre?"
"I would say that you learned your lessons well."
"And what do you say about the synchronicity of the retired judge who was born with a natural inclination to serve her community?"
"I would say that the logic of our dialectic is sound. You only need one more thing to bring this book to closure."
"What, pray tell?"
"The story with most conviction is the story of one's own life. You went out of your way to find your true self, and regardless how incredible your story may seem to the average reader it nonetheless rings true; so why not share your gift of being a messenger of sacred meaning? Tell us how you are personally called to serve the community of humanity."

"Off the top of my head, I can think of half a dozen times when I was called to meet a person's spiritual need for sacred meaning, the last time being when I was called to go to Barrie for Teresa DeCicco's book signing so I could write this book to satisfy my reader's need for sacred meaning. I never know why I am called to meet someone's need, but in the course of our conversation something always clicks, and before I know it I am telling the person what they need to hear to continue on their journey to wholeness and completeness, as I have been doing with this book. The second last time this happened, Penny and I were returning home from Thunder Bay where we had gone to visit Penny's sister, and on the way home I was strongly nudged to stop and visit Penny's sister's mother-in-law in the little hamlet of Dorion who had read some of my books and loved them. I had some of my new books in the car with us, and I was nudged to visit and give her a copy of *Why Bother? The Riddle of the Good Samaritan* and *Letters to Padre Pio*, but our visit was exactly what she needed, because she was in such a deep rut she didn't know what to do. The woman was eighty-seven years old, lived alone with a daughter close by, but for some reason she fell into despair and couldn't get herself out, which she pondered over her morning coffee; and just then we dropped in to visit. We had only intended to stay a few minutes, but I saw that her need for the special energy of sacred meaning that began to flow out of me the moment we sat down for tea overrode our need to get back on the road for our long journey home, and I just let 'it' pour out of me. And when she had enough sacred meaning to dispel her despair, she hugged me and whispered into my ear, 'I love you,' and Penny and I continued on our way home feeling good for our service."

"That was a beautiful moment, my friend. A beautiful moment."

"Thank you. As a matter of fact, I wrote a spiritual musing on my experience with this wonderful woman. Do you think I should include it to give the reader a taste of how the omniscient guiding principle of life works to help soul in its time of need?"

"By all means. It will be a beautiful capstone for our book"

"I think so too. Okay, here's my spiritual musing: —

Mrs. H's Wow Moment

In my spiritual musing *"The Synchronicity Principle"* I wrote: "I've come to believe that the *synchronicity principle* is set into motion by an all-knowing benevolent intelligence whose purpose is to guide every soul to wholeness and completeness," and last *Monday, September 14, 2015* I experienced the benevolence of this cosmic intelligence yet again in one of the most surprising synchronicities that I have ever experienced when Penny and I dropped in on Mrs. H on our way home from Thunder Bay where we had gone to visit Penny's sister.

It's a long drive from Thunder Bay to Georgian Bay and we had to stop in Nipigon to attend to some matters with our triplex apartment unit, so I had no intention of dropping in on Mrs. H who lived in a rural community on the Trans-Canada Highway midway between Thunder Bay and Nipigon, and we wanted to make it to Bruce Mines where we planned to get a motel room for the night and have dinner at Bobber's Restaurant where they served wonderful fresh fish and chips; but along the way I got the strongest nudge to drop in on Mrs. H and give her one or two of my books that we always carry in our car for complimentary give-aways.

Mrs. H is eighty-seven years old, and save for a curvature of the spine that makes walking difficult (she uses one of those walkers with wheels in her house), she's sound of mind and very curious about life; that's why she's taken to my writing, especially *Do We Have an Immortal Soul* that she loved so much she had to send it to one of her sons who was in the throes of a spiritual crisis.

She made a comment to me that I never forgot that spoke volumes about her life but which I never uncovered until last Monday when Penny and I dropped in to visit and give her a copy of *Letters to Padre Pio* and *Why Bother? The Riddle of the Good Samaritan*. I wanted to give her a copy of *The Pearl of Great Price*, but we only had one copy in the car and we had given that to Penny's lifelong friend in Thunder Bay; but the comment that

DEATH, THE FINAL FRONTIER

Mrs. H made to me years ago was: "When you have seen the light, there's no turning back." What an intriguing thing to say.

Obviously my first novel *What Would I Say Today If I Were to Die Tomorrow?* —which she read with eager fascination because it caused such a stir in my hometown that Penny and I had to relocate to Georgian Bay for peace of mind—had made such a strong impression upon her that she felt compelled to tell me about the effect that seeing the light can have upon people; but it never occurred to me to ask her how she had come to see the light that changed the course of her life; and that's what inspired today's spiritual musing, because within minutes of dropping in to visit Mrs. H she began to tell us the incredible story of her spiritual awakening...

Mrs. H has been a widow for quite some time, and she manages very nicely on her own; but she has a daughter and husband close by that she relies upon, and she called them to drop over because Penny and I were visiting.

We had only planned to stay a few minutes, but that turned into an hour and a half when her daughter and husband dropped over; but I didn't mind, because I knew by the nature of our conversation that divine synchronicity had choreographed our visit for Mrs. H's spiritual benefit, and also for her daughter's and husband's benefit as well because once my transcendent function has been engaged everyone in hearing distance is blessed with that special "something" that flows out of me.

I don't mean to sound mystical, but the transcendent function is an aspect of one's Higher Self; and since I've been a seeker all of my life who had the good fortune to find my true self, my transcendent function "kicks" in whenever I'm called upon to serve life because, as Elisabeth Kubler-Ross tells us in her autobiography *The Wheel of Life*, "all destiny leads down the same path—growth, love and service." That's why I was strongly nudged to drop in on Mrs. H on our way home to Georgian Bay, to serve her desperate need for more sacred meaning.

This is how divine synchronicity works; whenever someone is in need of spiritual guidance, the benevolent force of the universe activates the *synchronicity principle* to make it happen; and as I learned from our conversation, Mrs. H had slipped into a depressing funk and needed "something" to pick her up, which she was brooding about over her morning coffee as we were driving down the highway, and she could not get over the timely coincidence of us dropping in for a visit with two new books for her to read which were sure to raise her spirits, and the smile on her face said it all.

"This is my wow moment for the day," she said to her daughter, an expression I had never heard before but which I instantly discerned because it reflected beautifully what the writer Phil Cousineau called a "soul moment" in his book *Soul Moments, Marvelous Stories of Synchronicity—Meaningful Coincidences from a Seemingly Random World*. But what was Mrs. H's spiritual awakening experience that changed the course of her life? That's what she revealed to me...

Mrs. H only had a grade eight education, but she was naturally intelligent, inordinately curious, and musically gifted—qualities that she passed on to her eight children and grandchildren; but she was married to a man whose family belonged to a curious evangelical Christian sect called the *Two-by-Twos* (a name they got stuck with because they always evangelized from house to house in pairs), and Mrs. H's personal growth was gravely hampered by her husband's rigid faith.

Her husband worked for a department of the provincial government that was affiliated with the University of Guelph, and one day the Agricultural Department of the university had a guest speaker deliver a public lecture in Thunder Bay that Mrs. H and her husband and some fellow employees attended; but this lecture introduced Mrs. H to the radical concept of natural evolution that shattered her Christian belief that we are all decedents of Adam and Eve born with the stain of original sin, and she had such a startling spiritual awakening that shifted her never-before questioned belief in the Holy Bible that so threatened her husband's rigid faith that his family wanted to have Mrs. H committed to the Ontario Psychiatric Hospital in Thunder Bay.

This was a difficult time for Mrs. H, but she managed to survive in her marriage with her newfound perspective, and she became a life-long seeker; that's why when she read my novel *What Would I Say Today If I Were to Die Tomorrow?* many years later she was moved to say to me, "When you have seen the light, there's no turning back." Which is why she gave me a hug and whispered into my ear "I love you" when Penny and I got up to leave after our unexpected visit; it was her way of letting me know that she knew how difficult life can be when one has been spiritually awakened.

I smiled, and looking into her lively blue eyes so full of love and gratitude I said, "You're one of my favorite readers. This was a wow moment for me also, and I'm glad we dropped in for a visit. I hope you enjoy these books as much as the others."

"I know I will," she said, and Penny and I said our goodbyes and were back on the road to my hometown of Nipigon that caused us so much consternation, but I was delightfully satisfied in that special way that always happens whenever I'm called upon to serve life because we had left Mrs. H very happy.

———

Alright, Padre; I didn't think I would get to use it, but I have to now. I wrote a poem that captures this gift I have that will put this whole dialectic on the virtue of giving into classical perspective, and by this I mean the universal language of poetry that speaks to the soul. It would have sounded immodest without proper context, but I don't think so now. As I said, it has happened to me enough times in my life to know that I am used by *the omniscient guiding principle of life* to serve my fellow man with my gift of being open to the message of sacred meaning, and I'm certain now that my calling to write this book was a calling to give my readers what they need to know about their destined purpose. Well, here we are; and if my poem still has a lingering air of presumption, I apologize."

"Please, recite your poem and let the reader be the judge."

"Alright. Here's my poem: —

The Messenger

There's a calm tenacity to his words,
A power beyond endurance, but
so light are his thoughts to him that
he doesn't even notice.

When he speaks, he seems the same
as you and me; but at some point in
the conversation his demeanor changes,
and he's off to higher places.

Words flow from his mouth like fresh
spring water, and what was light,
easy, and ordinary now becomes
mystical with sacred meaning.

"It's like God sent you," they all say,
when he finishes speaking; and he smiles
and says, "I know. But that's what
you needed to hear, —"

And everything returns to normal.

"As with every poem that I write, I get the first line and then I have to work out the rest, and when my creative unconscious provided me with the line 'There's a calm tenacity to his words, a power beyond endurance,' I knew I had a poem that called to be written; and this speaks to the creative process and *the omniscient guiding principle of life*. But to be honest with you, Padre; I have no desire to expand upon this any further. Either one believes, or one does not; and the devil can have the hindmost."

DEATH, THE FINAL FRONTIER

"You are true to character, my friend. By all means, let the devil have the hindmost. After all, he too is part of God's Divine Plan."

"It's been a fascinating experience, Padre. Do you have any parting words?"

"Just one. Trust your readers. They're much wiser than you think."

"The eternal optimist! That's what I love about you, Padre. But didn't you tell me in one of my spiritual healing sessions that I trusted too much? That's why I got myself into the mess I did with that offshoot Christian solar cult teaching that did irreparable damage to my eyesight; but that's another story for another day…"

*****

About the Author

Born with a spiritual restlessness that could not be tamed by my Christian faith, I became a spiritual seeker when I discovered reincarnation in Plato's Dialogues at the age of fifteen. I grew up in a small town in Northwestern Ontario, and at twenty-one I had my own pool hall and vending machine business, but my restless spirit called me away to seek out my destiny, and I sold my business and sailed to France.

In the Alpine city of Annecy, in the Haute-Savoie region of France I had a dream that called me to my destiny. I entered into the mind of every person in the world and took every question they had ever asked and reduced them all to one question: *Why am I?* I returned to Canada and went to university to study philosophy to seek an answer to this haunting question, and by "chance" I discovered Gurdjieff, the redoubtable teacher of a system of transformative thought that he called "the Work." His Teaching excited my restless spirit and compelled me to seek out the answer to man's disquieting question in the fast, often tumultuous currents of daily living.

Visit him at: http://ostocco.wix.com/ostocco
Spiritual Musings Blog:
http://www.spiritualmusingsbyoreststocco.blogspot.com

ALSO BY OREST STOCCO

NOVELS

The Golden Seed
Tea with Grace
Jesus Wears Dockers
Healing with Padre Pio
Keeper of the Flame
My Unborn Child
On the Wings of Habitat
What Would I Say Today If I Were to Die Tomorrow?

NON-FICTION

Gurdjieff was wrong but his teaching works...
The Man of God Walks Alone
The Summoning of Noman
The Lion that Swallowed Hemingway
The Sum of All Spiritual Paths
Do We Have An Immortal Soul?
Stupidity Is Not a Gift of God
Letters to Padre Pio
Old Whore Life
Just Going with the Flow
Why Bother? The Riddle of the Good Samaritan
The Pearl of Great Price
In The Shade of the Maple Tree

www.ingramcontent.com/pod-product-compliance
Lightning Source LLC
LaVergne TN
LVHW011421080426
835512LV00005B/188